Being Black:
The Hard and The Cool

Keino Terrell

authorHOUSE®

AuthorHouse™
1663 Liberty Drive
Bloomington, IN 47403
www.authorhouse.com
Phone: 833-262-8899

Published by AuthorHouse 08/02/2022

ISBN: 978-1-4670-3937-6 (sc)
ISBN: 978-1-4670-3936-9 (hc)
ISBN: 978-1-4670-3935-2 (e)

Library of Congress Control Number: 2022914119

Print information available on the last page.

For Bryce, Kai, & Carter

CONTENTS

ACKNOWLEDGEMENTS

I offer a sincere thank you to my family, friends, and mentors for being my village. A special thank you to those that continue to serve Black folk with integrity, courage, and love.

PREFACE

As an undergraduate, I had the privilege of picking up Dr. Cornel West from the airport as he was on campus to deliver a speech for an event sponsored by the Black Student Union. I was also tapped from time to time to freelance for the university newspaper and the one-on-one time with the distinguished professor was the type of unique "Black Experience" that I was often asked to capture. Dr. West and I talked about a lot of things. He mentioned his son, who was attending a HBCU at the time, his debates with other Black intellectuals around the country, and he spent time asking me questions that made me feel as if he was genuinely interested in my dreams and desires. The way he called me "brother Keino" was settling, making me instantly at ease with a man I had admired for a long time. That hour or so we spent together in the car remains an important moment in my life, but he said something transformative during his presentation that evening.

As Dr. West, in his dark suit, white shirt, and black tie loose at the neck, worked the stage, he offered what he often does, an impeccable accounting of the history of Black folk and the crisis brought on by systemic racism in this country. But it was a line he delivered nearly halfway through his speech that got thundering applause from the Black folk in attendance, words that have resonated regularly with me over the years. He said, "Being Black may be hard– but it sure is cool."

This seemingly simple statement against some of the most linguistically sophisticated combinations of words I had ever heard perfectly captures my relationship with my Blackness. It is hard. And it is cool. And this combination of hard and cool has torn me down one day and helped me rise the next. Few would debate the challenges Black folk continue to face in a country designed to systematically stunt their educational, financial, and emotional growth. Systems that are designed with the sole purpose of protecting the existing power structure. Systems, be it housing, banking, the government, the courts, the legal system, schools, corporate America, or media and television, all work perfectly and coordinate to intentionally maintain and secure wealth, class, privilege, and advantage for white people.

But even in this race where white competitors get a head start and Black folk have to run backward before forwards, Black people seemingly have no desire to change places. This Black struggle has birthed a group of people that move differently, have a unique sound, and navigate life like the notes of a jazz song. And this, my friends, is cool. The type of cool that Dr. West was illuminating. A trend-setting kind of cool. An awe-inspiring type of cool. That Everyone wants to look like and be like you type of cool. A Black cool.

My journey and evolution as a Black man are as unique as it is ordinary. But, whereas my story is mine alone, this collective experience, this lived connectedness that we experience as Black folk, allows for a common truth when articulating the "hard" and celebrating the "cool." It is Ferguson and George Floyd just as much as it is Afros and Nina Simone. It is the terror of four little girls dying in a church bombing in Birmingham and Michael Jackson moonwalking across the Motown 25 stage in Detroit. It is the school-to-prison pipeline and step-shows by fraternities and sororities at Howard and North Carolina A & T. It is redlining and Jim Crow but also shell toe (top) Adidas with no laces and hoop earrings. We are these things and so much more.

Being Black is hard, and it is cool, and this juxtaposition, and the pain and joy inherent in it, takes a lifetime to reconcile. Yet, I am a Black man trying to understand my Blackness daily. I do so with tears in my eyes, and my Yankees cap tilted slightly to the side.

INTRODUCTION

Many years ago, I wrote a book with the hope that it would push forward specific types of conversations in the Black community. The intent was to be as much celebratory of who we are as Black folk as it was to be critical of the ways we were falling short. Unfortunately, the impact for some felt uneven and unfair. There was a desire to recognize the roles that systems play in creating the mentality of self-harm-- and harm to others– witnessed too often in our communities. Although discussions of systems of oppression are as frequent as conversations about the weather in Black households, it is important always to acknowledge that behaviors are influenced by history, both good and bad. This context and framing give appropriate respect to this truth. If the impact of my words hurt or damaged anyone, this is a regret I will carry with me always.

My views on race and humanity and my approach to diversity, equity, inclusion, and justice work continue to evolve as they should. Like most of you, I am also impacted by the thousands of new experiences and discussions about race surrounding us. I have unapologetically navigated Blackness in predominantly white environments for decades. I have done the work needed to understand further the trauma that racism has caused to me and those that share my identity and affinity. And importantly, I continue to be fully present in the search for solutions that will ultimately strengthen the community.

This book aims to forward new conversations about topics relevant to the Black experience and to reposition others. It is written in the spirit of unity and consistent with how I have lived my life, in constant partnership with those wishing to make a difference and improve things. It is an open invitation to those courageous enough to engage honestly about topics central to the Black experience and all of the layers and nuances this entails.

I'M COOL LIKE THAT

I'm cool like that, I'm proud like that, and I'm a Black man like that
The more things change, the more they stay the same
Whenever there's a crime, it's me that they blame
I'm more than an athlete or the latest rap lyricist
It's my intelligence, perseverance, and contributions that they miss
The image of the gangster or the womanizer, I keep out of sight
Instead, I teach my kids about those who fought for our civil rights
I can be anything, and by now, this should be evident
For more proof, take a look at the 44th President
Because I'm cool like that, I'm proud like that, and I'm a Black man like that

SYSTEMS

"Just like freedom, Truth is not cheap. Yet both are worth more than all the gold in the world. But what is freedom, if there is no truth? And what is truth, if there is no freedom? Both are worth fighting for — because one without the other would be hell." — Suzy Kassem

&

"Racism is so universal in this country, so widespread, and deep-seated, that it is invisible because it is so normal." — Shirley Chisholm

CHAPTER 1

◆

SYSTEMS

My first real lesson in systemic racism came when I was very young, and I overheard a conversation between my mom and dad about "The Man." My dad, who worked two full-time jobs my entire childhood, eagerly hoping to start his own asphalt paving business, was lamenting how Black folk got charged higher interest rates on bank loans. This was, of course, if they even got approved for a loan. My mom's contribution to my education was helping me to understand that "The Man" that my father was referencing was no one white man specifically. White people, in general enjoyed certain advantages in life because they controlled things. In other words, they held power and were in positions to stack the deck in their favor in most situations, mainly when this pitted them against a Black person.

As I aged and my thinking became more sophisticated, I made the appropriate connection that "The Man," popular terminology with Black folk back in the day, was synonymous with what we now label as systems of oppression. These systems, be it education, government, banking, housing, and even culture, all work to support and reinforce the oppression of marginalized groups. In this country, the most marginalized group is perhaps Black people because of the ugly role of enslavement. Centuries of free labor and the accumulation of wealth and property during this time are still the number one variable of note in understanding the generational wealth gap between Black and white folk. Couple this with an intentional campaign to dehumanize Black folk as a justification for such horrific treatment and a better understanding of why systems were created and how they protect certain privileges is gained.

Few are proud of this country's history of oppression. But what is equally shameful is that we have an uncanny understanding of how systems work today, yet we struggle to disrupt them to balance the lived experience between Black and white people. Black folk are still paid less money than white folk to do the same jobs and are far less likely to hold executive positions even when better educated and have more experience. Property in predominantly Black neighborhoods consistently receives lower appraisals, compromising the ability to use home equity as a strategy for further wealth creation. Educational funding connects to property taxes, and as Black people tend to live in areas that generate fewer tax dollars, schools are often lacking from those found in and funded by predominately white neighborhoods. Blacks receive longer jail sentences for the same illegal activities as white perpetrators, and even a "Black" sounding" name can mean the difference between getting a job interview or not.

The consequence of these intricate overlapping structures that limit Black folk is that racism becomes more difficult to prove and challenge. It often becomes less explicit or readily visible. It can almost seem hidden and protected in sophisticated ways. For example, the legal system's penalty for selling marijuana impacts young Black males disproportionately. Not only are they found guilty more regularly, but they also receive longer sentences compared to their white counterparts. Is the activity of selling drugs illegal? Sure. But the impact and domino effect of the conviction is felt in Black households where this person is removed for more extended periods from home and then unable to find suitable work once they are out.

Over the last decade, the study of racism has focused on systems, and rightfully so. However, for real change to happen, at least the type that is sustainable, Black folk must be truly afforded the same opportunity for success in all facets of life as white folk. Equity requires removing the privilege and advantage that white people enjoy that is hidden in the systems. Students receiving admission to the best colleges because of lineage, closed-door job offers, and promotions protected by the idea of "fit" must go. Banks giving Black applicants with the same credit profile as white applicants higher interest rates on a mortgage or business loan must also go away. Health care that sees Black patients die disproportionately compared to white patients with a similar illness, and school districts that routinely overlook Black students for advanced classes and leadership opportunities must no longer exist. And even standards of beauty that compromise Black folk because of hair texture or style must all be dismantled as they limit Black folk while protecting the advantages of white folk whether they want this advantage or not.

Indeed, the study of systems, how they work, and how they can be challenged and destroyed must remain a focus, but also note that system changes happen slowly. There's also no guarantee that any change to any of the systems mentioned will happen in my lifetime. They may never happen. For Black folk, this reality has always been abundantly clear. White folk will need to willingly give up power, advantage, and privilege to bring about significant change to systems. They must be willing to level the playing field so that their children have no inherited edge to securing college placement, a job, a loan on a home, or wealth. Mainly, white folk must admit that these systems and these advantages that come with them exist. Many deny this.

My point is that we must continue to work on solutions to improve the lived experiences of Black folk now, even as we fight like hell for criminal justice reform, voting rights, better policing, and other structures that support racial equality. What is perilous in some conversations about systemic oppression is that we think that naming the system that causes injustice makes life better for those oppressed daily. It does not. Or that one particular strategy can dismantle any structure. It can not. The truth is that the same systems of oppression that we speak of today as needing to change are the same ones my parents and grandparents talked about in years past. I am also reasonably sure that these systems I discuss with my boys will be the ones they also address with their children. Systems change is unhurried and incremental. Telling a young person that they may have to wait nearly a lifetime for some measure of noticeable change sometimes feels cruel and unfair.

My last real lesson on systemic racism came during a recent conversation with a white person at a diversity training I attended. During a discussion on race centered on Black folk, they told me that as they had grown up in a relatively impoverished Black neighborhood and attended predominantly Black schools, they also felt discriminated against and disenfranchised most of their life. The actual cost of systemic oppression for me is that often I think that I don't even get to have ownership of my own experience.

What's Hard: may takes generations or never change, requires white folk to surrender privilege, impacts Black folk from birth to death

What's Cool: being able to explain that oppression is protected, the possibilities that come when systems are disrupted

BLACK EXCELLENCE

"Those who say it can't be done are usually interrupted by others doing it." — James Baldwin

&

"I was raised to believe that excellence is the best deterrent to racism or sexism. And that's how I operate my life." — Oprah Winfrey

CHAPTER 2

BLACK EXCELLENCE

Several years ago, I had an interesting conversation with a friend as the concept of Black excellence was gathering momentum across Black Twitter and other social media platforms. You might remember some of these postings of Black folk shining bright and demonstrating our brilliance, creativity, intelligence, artistic ability, community engagement, and desire and willingness to transform the world for the better. Black excellence was absolute, with our standards and metrics being used to determine what fit and did not fit. My friend was the epitome of Black excellence, in my opinion. She was a Ph.D., a Spellman graduate, made lots of money, was highly respected in her profession, and mentored countless Black professionals across the country. I witnessed her speak truth to power whenever needed, even when the consequence to her was severe.

What confused me was that she would push back against the concept of Black excellence because, from her perspective, celebrating the idea somehow felt divisive to Black folk failing to meet a certain bar or standard. She was so worried about how her struggling brothers and sisters might feel she was willing to dim the light of Black folk demonstrating excellence around her. She did not want to celebrate, honor, promote, encourage, or even normalize what they were doing if this meant that others might feel less. It was even difficult for her to speak the words *Black Excellence*.

This brilliant and empathetic young woman also disrupted some of my thinking on Black excellence. Not that I shouldn't acknowledge Black excellence. It should be shouted from the rooftops when witnessed. But honoring Black excellence required balance and thoughtfulness, just as my criticism of those not yet finding their excellence needed to be measured and given with care. My earlier writing around this topic was too binary. Perhaps even too harsh. Despite my intention to point out and prepare young people for unfair future evaluations and where excellence will be required to open doors, this message must be delivered with surgical precision so as not to extinguish the light in the belly of a single Black person.

Engaging with Black excellence has always been a constant in my life. I seek it out in what I read and watch, storing examples away in my mental Rolodex to whip out like flashcards with my boys whenever necessary. It even seems that my mother believes it is her job to send me videos and articles of random Black people reaching magnificent achievements or milestones. She does this not only because she finds joy and pride in their excellence but hopes that these examples continue to feed my drive and that of her grandchildren.

But there are other dimensions to the conversation of Black excellence that I have with my close friends. Conversations littered with nuances fitting of mention here. These highly successful Black folk speak of the pressures associated with Black excellence. The internal battle to constantly be the smartest in the room, the best at the job, the one representing the community and other Black folks that may follow, the one chosen to change the educational and financial trajectory of a family for generations to come. The weight of Black excellence can be overwhelming and even debilitating at times. Consider that many places you work when you are Black and excellent aren't always where you are wanted or understood. Sites that may not be the most diverse. You may be surrounded by people who are intimidated by this excellence. Jealous of this excellence. Skeptical of this excellence. Even places where people deliberately and hatefully work to tarnish this excellence. Yet this excellence must be on full display always.

The value of having examples of Black excellence is unquestionable. It is vital to a community and any group of people needing to counter violent images and support young people's dreams. However, it is necessary to evolve in our thinking of how this is discussed in our community, to continue to search for the light of excellence in all people, and to offer care and encouragement to those who provide us with the examples we use with our kids. Black excellence comes with significant pressure. It requires that we protect people as much as we preserve the concept.

What's Hard: pressure to be perfect, imposter syndrome, family & community burden

What's Cool: lifeline to advancement, actualizing ancestors dreams, Oprah & Labron

THE N-WORD

"I noticed that among this class of colored men the word "nigger" was freely used in about the same sense as the word "fellow," and sometimes as a term of almost endearment; but I soon learned that its use was positively and absolutely prohibited to white men."
— James Weldon Johnson,

&

"I believe that a speaker's intention is what gives a word its power. And if we eliminate the N word, other words would just take its place." —Jay-Z

CHAPTER 3

THE N-WORD

During my 25 years working in education in different positions, I have been on too many committees to count that admirably tried to come up with an N-word policy for school that seemed both fair and thoughtful. An approach that could get at what the school truly wanted to achieve. Many of these committees happened before a more informed discussion differentiating equity from equality. Consequently, most of these committees dissolved, failing to accomplish what they set out to do.

One committee failed because committee members could not find a pathway to address the N-word found in the literature and some primary sources used in classes. How can we censor great texts, someone would argue? Or are kids not going to read *The Tales of Huckleberry Finn* or *To Kill a Mockingbird*? Some educators initially equated the mere suggestion of removing these "Classics" with academic malpractice. For some, this was the fight that was worthy of no compromise.

As time progressed, discussions about the N-word graduated from whether connotations of the word change when ending with an "a" or "er." Next, schools considered if white students could use the word if they were singing a rap song or if they could say the word if they received a pass from a Black student. Then there was zero tolerance for all students and no reading the word aloud if it came up in class. Finally, schools even started removing any policy from the handbook in exchange for what the community would practice regarding the N-word. As a result, today, the only thing consistent about N-word policies is no consistency.

It seems strange, but it has only been in the last handful of years that we have applied the idea of equity vs. equality to the use of the N-word in schools. Perhaps we always have in some ways but not in a manner that could be explained satisfactorily or consistently in all settings. Equity requires that schools allow Black students to navigate the N-word differently than white students. Equality would mean that all students, regardless of race and relationship to the word, are held to the same standard, with consequences distributed evenly.

Schools quickly learned that the complexity of Black folk's relationship with the N-word is a school policy nightmare. The word lives in most buildings on campus. You hear it during sporting events and evening socials. But, frankly, any teacher may stumble upon a conversation involving Black students at any point of the day, and the N-word may resonate. So what are schools to do when the N-word lives so differently in the lives of Black folk than it does and should for white people?

In *Us vs. Them*, I manipulated the use of the N-word in a manner that some found challenging at best and offensive at worst. Most, however, tried to understand how redefining the word, not necessarily to remove its power, was being utilized to explore mentality. In retrospect, going for the provocative to force conversation was folly and worked contrary to the ultimate goal of having people emotionally available to engage. Instead, some struggled to settle their demons with the word to make space for the more difficult discourse that the book demands. When I tell people that I haven't uttered the N-word in some 25 years but wrote a book using it so often, this further solidifies how personal its use is to each Black person. It also underscores why policy and even practice concerning the word can feel so loaded, complicated, unfair, and frustrating.

The truth is that some Black people use the word daily and are entirely comfortable with this decision. They are no less pro-black, just at peace with the myriad ways the word manifests in their lives. They may be entertained by its inclusion in music, stand-up comedy, cable tv dramas, books, and social settings. Yet, some Black people are uncomfortable anywhere and under any circumstance if the word is used around them. They may connect the word only to a painful past and may be unwilling or unable to move from this space.

But many Black people fall somewhere on this spectrum, comfortable sometimes and not others. People impacted greatly by the demographics of those around them when the word comes up, the mood they are in at that moment, their age, or any other variables that may be relevant to them at any given time and in any given place. The truth is that there is no consensus on the use of the word for Black folk. Each reserves the right and is deserving of this unique relationship.

However, there is remarkable consistency in that Black people have no tolerance for white people using the N-word or participating in discourse about the appropriateness of its usage. Many of my white friends have struggled with this over the years, genuinely wanting to understand how any Black person would dare use a word with such a dubious history. A word that, if delivered from the lips of a person with less pigmentation, conjures visions of lynchings, white gowns, and hoods. A word used to demonize and demoralize generations of Black folk. Many white folks still hold the word like a concealed weapon at the ready if they deem it time to inflict harm.

These wonders by white folk are entirely understandable. However, I sometimes question if white peoples' frustration with Black folk's use of the N-word has more to do with some perceived double standard or even their discomfort that the word somehow gives Black folk power or privilege over them. I am the first to admit that the N-word usage is confusing. But the reality is that Black folk have reclaimed the word, reconfigured it, removed some of its power by manipulating context, and are comfortable with its usage being messy, complicated, and ever-evolving. This explanation may be unsatisfactory to white people and even some Black people, but the N-word remains a permanent fixture in the Black vernacular.

What's Hard: no community consensus, connection to history of white hate

What's Cool: full ownership, agency to define and alter its meaning, unapologetically messy

HIP-HOP MUSIC

"Hip-hop is about the brilliance of pavement poetry."
— Michael Eric Dyson

&

"Hip-hop is very diverse, but if you only focus on one aspect of it, then what you get is this image of Black America that is completely contrary to what actually goes on." — Prince

CHAPTER 4

HIP-HOP MUSIC

Is it possible to love and hate the same thing simultaneously? If so, this perfectly describes my relationship with rap music. When I heard *The Message* by Grandmaster Flash and the Furious Five, I became addicted to an art form that could be so vulnerable, brutally honest, captivating, and creative in telling the stories of people growing up in similar situations to my own. The mirrors to my life found in the music were like a drug, with me hanging on every expertly arranged metaphor, rhyming couplet, and punchline. How could something so raw be so beautiful?

In rap's infancy, it never seemed to disappoint. The Sugarhill Gang's *Rapper's Delight* added a party dimension to the genre, and the song made the music available to a broader audience. The '80s gave us Run DMC, The Beastie Boys, Doug E. Fresh, LL Cool J, and Slick Rick. Slick Rick's *Hey Young World* provided a small glimpse into how the music could be used for teaching and serving young people. And although rap always revealed characteristics of inflated masculinity and sexual performance hyperbole, these things were secondary to what was becoming the signature platform to youthful Black expression—a front row seat to Black urban life.

When NWA hit the scene in the late 80s, it did not only announce to the world that rap, which started in New York, had reached the country's west coast but had expanded and evolved. Gangsta rap and in-your-face, violent, tell it like it is, profanity-laced, and far more vulgar style of music captivated audiences. The anti-police, anti-authority, and anti-establishment messages were not that different from what Public Enemy was shouting in *Fight the Power*. But NWA's unfiltered language, gang affiliations, and demands that America respects their first amendment protection of free speech created lots of fear and criticism from white folk who were now paying attention to the sounds permeating their suburban homes and neighborhoods.

By the mid-90s, talk of rap being some fad was now laughable, and as music sales started to outpace all other genres, rap artists became household names, and hip-hop culture became more marketable. It played well on television and the big screen. Will Smith, LL Cool J, and Queen Latifah had leading roles in weekly sitcoms, and Kid 'n Play, Tupac Shakur, DMX, and Ice-Cube found themselves walking the red carpet. And when Three 6 Mafia shockingly won the Oscar for best song with *It's Hard Out Here for a Pimp*, it was a sign that Hollywood elites embraced the music. It was not to be ignored in spaces representing the highest levels of performance and artistry.

But even as rap music was having massive financial success, with its crossover appeal having united groups of people across racial barriers, what was also apparent was that the socially conscious aspects of the music had faded. Groups like A Tribe Called Quest, Public Enemy, Dead Prez, and artists like Mos Def, Lauren Hill, and Tupac Shakur were becoming more difficult to find. The 2000s saw radio play dominated by songs that were still lyrically impressive but with an abundance of celebration of wealth, violence, and misogyny. The "bling" error and all of the images of fancy cars, duffle bags of cash, and massive mansions, were only outpaced by the continuation of the sexualization of women. The success of Lil' Kim and her bold lyrics and willingness to expose her body was in many ways empowering and needed to open doors for female rappers. But it also created a blueprint that Trina, Nicki Minaj, Cardi B, and Megan Thee Stallion would follow—and that rely heavily on explicit sexual content to compete in a male-dominated industry.

The result is that hundreds of rappers glorify violence, and female artists have one pathway to success. For every Common, J Cole, and Kendrick Lamar, that create music to challenge destructive practices to Black folk and celebrate the concept of Blackness, far too many songs celebrate illegal drug activity and the degradation of women. Unfortunately, these songs seem to gain traction and popularity and dominate radio playlists and downloads. More troublesome is that many people believe that the characters and personas that many rap artists take on in their music are true. These violent and fictitious stories they tell further desensitize us to the violence in our neighborhoods.

Rap music is no more responsible for the violence in our community than any other type of music, gangsta movies, or television series found on many streaming platforms. Watching Netflix's Squid Game, one of the most violent series ever created, did not lead to an uptick in murder, nor did it convince anyone to embrace any of the despicable behaviors of the characters. Squid Game was viewed through a lens of entertainment with no confusion as to whether the show's events were true. The problem is that rap was built on something different. It was supposed to be true. But the authenticity that attracted me to the music so long ago seems to have faded.

Perhaps there is one thing that could sustain my love for rap music. For more artists like Jay-Z to be comfortable saying that what is being offered in the music is not true but fabrications. That rap songs are stories no different from what we find when we turn on the tv. Most songs and the lives depicted in videos are not to take literally. That life is not meant to imitate art. Sure, Jay-Z, the billionaire, finds himself in a position where he can make this distinction without harming his career or bank account. For others, rich only for the duration of their four-minute music video, this statement of lack of authenticity would most likely be career-ending. I understand this dilemma.

Hip-Hop music has opened the door to financial and artistic success for many young Black folks. In addition, rap is a platform for discovering some of the greatest poets of this generation. However, its evolution depends solely on what those in positions of power want to package as authentic and how far artists will push power structures to support and invest in rappers that capture a broader range of the Black experience.

What's Hard: glorification of violence, overly sexualized, misogyny, relationship with LGBTQ community

What's Cool: word play and creation, lyrical poetry, unifying quality, power of platform, Black wealth creation

BLACK LIVES MATTER

"I can't make people not afraid of black people. I don't know what's going on. I can't explain what's happening in your head. But maybe if I show up every day as a human, a good human, doing wonderful things, loving my family, loving your kids, taking care of things that I care about—maybe, just maybe that work will pick away at the scabs of your discrimination."–Michelle Obama

&

"Racism is not getting worse, it's getting filmed."
— Will Smith

CHAPTER 5

BLACK LIVES MATTER

While sitting in my living room watching the horrific Sandy Hook Elementary School shooting news unfold, something felt different about the discussion about the need for restrictive gun legislation. Certainly, the deaths of so many innocent young children at the hands of a maniac carrying an automatic weapon would warrant such change, even for those card-carrying NRA members and hunters. Moreover, the visuals of the 20 young children and six adults that plastered screens for weeks would undoubtedly be pivotal in the debate about gun control and violence. Right?

Years later, I sat in an identical spot in my living room as the video of George Floyd's murder played on loop across media stations. His large body, seemingly diminished by the three officers kneeling on his back and neck. This treatment of Floyd resulted from his paying for an item in a corner store with a counterfeit twenty-dollar bill. His words, barely audible, begged the officers for air and finally called for help from his mother. Those who had gathered at the scene in the Minneapolis neighborhood also asked the officers for mercy and grace, pleading with them to reduce the pressure on Floyd's body and show him some humanity. But the white police officer, Derek Chauvin, continued to kneel on Floyd's neck for more than 9 minutes, several coming after he had stopped breathing. This senseless killing of George Floyd would undoubtedly be the moment of racial reckoning in the United States. Right?

My first memory of the Black Lives Matter slogan was after the death of Travon Martin in 2012. His death at the hands of a neighborhood watch person, George Zimmerman, came as he returned home from the store where he purchased some candy and a drink. Much talk followed about Florida's ridiculous stand your ground laws and the fear associated with Black boys wearing hoodies. But what Black folk wanted front and center was recognition of law enforcement's harm to black and brown bodies. The cry that Black lives matter was a way to force white folk to see Black people as fully human, with lives and loved ones the same as them. That the slogan, Black Lives Matter, even needed to be offered further testified to the racial inequity still experienced in the country. Black folk would need to explicitly state that there is a cost to killing them, that they feel unseen and unheard and unconsidered, and that there needs to be accountability and consequence when police kill them.

These reminders to white folk about the humanity of Black people are not new. We saw similar statements like "I am a man" on signs held by peaceful protesters throughout the Civil Rights Movement. Indeed, civil rights were mainly about securing and protecting our humanity. That Black lives matter and desegregation, voting rights, and housing security were necessary for this to be true. White folk understood that the Black man holding the sign was, in fact, a man, but what was missing was that he did not feel like one because his life lacked care, empathy, and consideration from those in power. A feeling of being incomplete stripped him of his humanity, which became reinforced through daily racist and discriminatory encounters with his oppressor.

Even today, white people know that Black lives matter, but counter-slogans like "All Lives Matter" or "Blue Lives Matter" further demonstrate a lack of understanding of the Black experience. The lived experience of Black folk, who face daily microaggressions and insults, profiling and questionable policing, and other discriminatory practices is often challenging conceptually. That I, a highly educated and professional Black man with no criminal record, am still followed in stores and subject to unwarranted police stops correlates with my feeling that my life may not matter as much as others.

When I discuss Black Lives Matter with white folk, Black on-Black crime is inevitably raised as a source of confusion. Some question how a slogan committed to the protection of Black bodies completely ignores what is happening in Chicago, Detroit, Atlanta, Philadelphia, and other large cities. What of Black folk killing other Black folk at alarming numbers and with seemingly little care or concern for the larger premise of the movement? They further wonder why there are no large-scale protests like what transpired across the country after the deaths of Mike Brown, Tamir Rice, Sandra Bland, Breanna Taylor, and George Floyd when so many, particularly young Black males, are getting gunned down daily.

This disconnect is understandable, and I get why this is hard for some white people to reconcile. However, the Black Lives Matter Movement is about looking at the issue of policing and the lack of training of law officers that make them more apt to use deadly force in encounters with Black males than with others. It highlights how personal and unconscious bias impacts those who must make split-second decisions about using deadly force or not. It is presumptuous to tell the organizers of Black Lives Matter to change its goal because there are other related issues that should be of concern. Is this the standard we hold for all social justice-oriented organizations?

Moreover, to understand Black-on-Black crime, it is best not to remove it from an analysis of the factors that lead to all crime. That includes white-on-white crime. And in using the phrase, it is essential to understand that its origin helped to justify more policing in Black communities and ultimately led to increased incarceration rates of Black folk. Consider the increase in Black incarceration during President Ronald Reagan's war on drugs in the '80s and the "super predators" and "three-strike" language of the Clintons in the '90s. The crime challenges in Black urban communities require improved education, better-paying jobs, investment in businesses in these communities, a sounder Black family structure, and a reversal of systems that lead some to low self-worth and hopelessness.

The takeaway is that lives of Black folk matter always, yet a focus on policing reform in this country is not only warranted but well overdue. Doing so does not discredit the policing profession, the bravery required to do a difficult job, or the appreciation we all feel when law enforcement serves the public good. Instead, I submit that we use every opportunity possible to lift up Black folk's humanity and do so without judgment but with grace. Like the tragedy at Sandy Hook Elementary School did not move the needle on gun legislation, George Floyd's death and the protests and conversations about Black lives following, may not change policing of Black folk in the moments that matter most.

What's Hard: distraction from issue of equitable policing, crime increases encounters with police, laws that protect police misconduct, unwarranted criticism of police

What's Cool: transparency of police body cameras, community/policing partnership, initiatives for increased diversity on police force

WHITE ALLIES

"For to be free is not merely to cast off one's chains, but to live in a way that respects and enhances the freedom of others." — Nelson Mandela

&

"No matter how big a nation is, it is no stronger than its weakest people, and as long as you keep a person down, some part of you has to be down there to hold him down, so it means you cannot soar as you might otherwise." — Marian Anderson

CHAPTER 6

———◆———

WHITE ALLIES

As part of a diversity exercise, I would ask white folk to write their ten closest friends' names and racial identities. After realizing that most people of a certain age no longer have ten close friends, I would reduce the number to seven. It is essential to clarify that by friends, I meant those that frequently visit your home, you eat out with them, and maybe even vacation. I have found that white people live highly isolated lives from Black folk, even those who are politically more liberal and those working to be anti-racist. Why this is so is less important to me than what must happen to reverse this reality. I make this point because allyship requires authentic relationships, ones where actions and words are congruent. For white allies to honestly do the necessary work, they must place themselves in situations where the names of a few Black folk can make it on the list.

At some point, Black folk seemed serious about putting the onus on white people to deal with their racism. They were done with pleading, begging, teaching, and even threatening white people to address what was considered their mess. However, for white people to do what was required, a large segment would need to step forward to become better informed at leading conversations about privilege, bias, white fragility, and systemic oppression with all of their friends and families. That meant uncomfortable discussions at home, at family gatherings, and workplace. White folk would even need to start having affinity group meetings where they unpack the concept of whiteness, something many had never considered.

In my experience, the idea of privilege has been the most difficult for white folk to reconcile. Perhaps this is because no one wants to believe they have had an unfair advantage over others. It is hard to accept that what I have worked hard to accomplish may have been assisted by something as superficial as skin color. Even certain achievements, job offers, and promotions may have come partly from bias. I understand why pushing back against this way of thinking is helpful. Explaining to your kids, partner, family, and friends that a position at work you coveted since joining the company many years ago may have come to fruition not only because of performance but because of a system that has always favored those like you is hard to do.

Conversations concerning privilege are difficult for most white people because it requires admitting to certain advantages that most had no part in creating. For white folk, privilege is an inherited right built into the country's fabric and protected by institutions that favor them above all others. This is not to suggest that all white folk reach high levels of success because of this privilege or that effort and hard work are not essential elements of achievement. White privilege does not guarantee an easy life or an excellent education. White folk suffer from poor schooling, poverty, and abuse, just like other races. However, the job of white allies is to give voice to the idea that privilege is forever present in the systems, even though not every white person advances from it. For comparison, there is successful Black folk despite a system that works against them.

White allies have helped call out racism and discriminatory practices in all spaces. A job usually reserved for people of color on location, now white allies speak out against racism, pushing their organizations to be anti-racist. This is essential for white allies to do publicly and privately but requires continuously educating themselves about how racism is present in the language used and practices considered normal. Identifying racism as it is happening, calling it out, and then disrupting it has strengthened the relationship between white allies and Black folk.

As the work of white allies continues to evolve, it will be important that progress happens in a couple of areas. The first is that white allies continue to listen carefully to the experiences of Black folk, so they feel empowered to share these experiences with other white people. When effective listening happens, and white allies repeat these sentiments, Black folk retain ownership of their positions and perceptions. White people often engage in the infuriating and frustrating practice of telling Black folk how they should feel and navigate their Blackness. White allies help by pointing out this harmful action and naming that it is white privilege that makes them think it is appropriate.

Another way that white allies can assist Black folk is by supporting, defending, and promoting Black people when possible. By sharing power and positions with Black folk and by using their privilege in support of empowering the voices of Black people, white allies work against white supremacy and close the opportunity gap. For example, there is significant value in white allies demanding more diversity in the workplace, especially in spaces where decision-making is happening. When Black folk get excluded from these meetings, so are their perspectives and experiences, increasing the likelihood that what gets decided will not be in their best interest. White allies naming those not in the room force white people to consider the consequence of this absence.

There is no doubt that white allies' role in race relations has increased in importance and sophistication. Look at the number of books that consider white fragility, tears, fears, and racial conditioning. This education is encouraging as the load carried teaching white folk about racism is substantial. It is also crucial that white people hold each other accountable for racist behavior and work to destroy the systems that give them unmatched power and advantage.

What's Hard: anti-racist framework still developing, building trust, sustaining the work, building authentic relationships with Black folk

What's Cool: white accountability, unpacking whiteness, positioning the destruction of racism where it belongs

Author's Note

The following topics remain central to the Black experience in this country. It is essential to remove any noise that would prevent digesting the aspirational intent of the words. Although works in progress, we as Black folk have power over our destiny, but unless we believe this to be true, we find ourselves beholden to others to determine our fate. What would it look and feel like to be our best selves? What may be possible for our children, family, and community?

> "Impossible is just a big word thrown around by small men who find it easier to live in the world they've been given than to explore the power they have to change it. Impossible is not a fact. It's an opinion. Impossible is not a declaration. It's a dare. Impossible is potential. Impossible is temporary. Impossible is nothing." —Muhammad Ali

EDUCATION

"We will all, at some point, encounter hurdles to gaining access and entry, moving up and conquering self-doubt; but on the other side is the capacity to own opportunity and tell our own story." — Stacey Abrams

&

"Education is our passport to the future, for tomorrow belongs to the people who prepare for it today." — Malcolm X

CHAPTER 7

EDUCATION

Ask any successful person who has managed to pull himself up from less than desirable circumstances, and he will tell you that the key to his accomplishment came from education. Yet, already I hear the cynics yelling, "What about the athletes and the entertainers?" Ok, some are lucky enough to play a professional sport or sign a lucrative recording contract, but the odds of hitting that lottery are similar to those of being struck by lightning. Also, remember that most professional athletes go to college, and nearly all have at least finished high school.

At some point, our views on education have become askew, with the worst case being that in some predominantly Black communities, the dropout rate of 50% seems normal. As a result, many students demonstrate a low learning capacity and even less desire to try. There are many contributors to this disheartening dilemma; parents who are rarely home because of work; parents who are incapable of assisting with the schoolwork; inadequate facilities, insufficiently trained teachers, and even a student's fear of failure. However, the history of Black folk in this country reveals that these prohibitive factors have always been present. You could argue that the obstacles faced by young people in the past were far more daunting and imposing than what students have today. In the past, students had to drop out to assist their families financially and navigated several miles to and from school. Facilities and supplies, both at school and in-home, would be laughable by today's standards. Teachers were younger and far less experienced, and the information about learning differences was nonexistent. Parents could not assist with the learning because many never came close to finishing school.

Nonetheless, the Black community actively sought education, making it the centerpiece and foundation for the future. Parents sacrificed what little they had to further their child's education; in return for this sacrifice, the child vowed to do her best. Older siblings set the example for younger siblings, and failure to do well-brought shame to the entire family. The community embraced academic success, the spirit of academic competition, and the desire to help others advance. This spirit resonated for what seemed like generations. There was a sense of togetherness. The success of one person was shared by all, while the failure of one person was enough to destroy the community.

Black folk still see education as the cornerstone of success in this country. They sacrifice time, energy, and money to give their children the best opportunity to do well. They invest in writing tutors for the children or SAT preparation courses instead of the newest iPhone and find ways to be active in their children's schooling. Black folk keep in touch with teachers, show up on curriculum night, limit the amount of television and internet time, supplement the school curriculum with other lessons at home, and let their children know they care. Black folk hold their children accountable for poor grades and reward excellence. Doing well is described in the house as expected. Less is unwelcomed.

Black folk model the behaviors that they demand from their children. For example, if they want their children to read, they read themselves. If they want their children to be responsible for completing schoolwork, they show discipline at their jobs and home duties. They monitor how they speak if they want their children to be articulate. Awards, degrees, and academic achievements are displayed in prominent places around the house, and conversations about future goals are often discussed. Black folk check homework regularly, and even if they cannot help the children to understand the work better, they keep abreast of the progress. They ensure that the assignment is at least complete and check with the teacher when their children continuously come home confused.

Black folk understand that their children must be able to compete in the knowledge market. Through experience, they may have learned that their children may need to be better than their white counterparts to have a chance at a spot at a top university or a position at a job. This competitiveness drives Black folk. They are anxious to demonstrate their intellect at school and at home. Black children have a fantastic ability to adapt. One moment they may speak to a friend in a broken dialect littered with the latest street jargon. The next, enunciating on the phone or to a teacher with the fluency of a linguistics teacher. Black children strive for good grades and ignore anyone or anything that attempts to derail them. When made fun of for their academic excellence, they wipe away the criticism like sweat, allowing haters to hate. They encourage their friends to do well, offer help when needed, surround themselves with the best and brightest, and believe that excellence loves company.

Black children often read a book or study school notes on the bus. They are the ones that are not allowed to the party if a big assignment is due. Yet, they are the ones who volunteer for everything, who will try anything, who will sacrifice all to advance themselves. Black children organize study groups, pull all-nighters, challenge teachers to create a better curriculum, and complete what they start. They have opinions on everything and a thirst for knowledge as a marathon runner for water. They are creative, athletic, and honest with themselves about their strengths and weaknesses. As a result, they win awards, get acknowledged at graduation, and accept scholarships. Black children shine.

Black children are unique because although they may not come from the most ideal of circumstances, they understand that they have the power to determine their destiny. Even when worrying about completing a school assignment seems less significant than the troubles that consume them at home, they find a way to do that which will ultimately change their lives. They know that hard work and dedication will open doors to a world that embraces and celebrates the educated. They know that by becoming educated, they will be able to help their families and other Black children who face similar struggles of poor resources and teachers who may no longer care. Black children ignore anyone claiming that success is a matter of luck. They are convinced they are responsible for creating good or bad fortune. They bet on themselves and always win.

What's Hard: balancing school with difficult home life, complicated learning profiles, unsafe schools, unresponsive teachers

What's Cool: most direct line to success, broadens perspective, provides hope and opportunity, wealth creation

Author's Note: Education remains the most direct line to upward mobility and the capacity to determine life's trajectory for Black folk. Unfortunately, Black students continue to face an uphill battle in closing achievement gaps with white students. Resources that support better educational outcomes highly correlate with social status creating even more challenges for the Black community. However, technology and the availability of information are being utilized in significant ways in homes and in communities to combat problems with overcrowded classrooms, an average 3 to 1 spending ratio deficit, inferior teaching quality, and environments that are not conducive to learning. We must keep Black children and families fully invested in educational pathways regardless of the obstacles. Schools remain the institution that provide the best opportunities for the greatest number of Black folk to succeed.

IMAGE

"I am no longer accepting the things I cannot change. I am changing the things I cannot accept." — Angela Y. Davis

&

"If the only time you think of me as a scientist is during Black History Month, then I must not be doing my job as a scientist." — Neil deGrasse Tyson

CHAPTER 8

IMAGE

The Black community, more so than any other, is in a constant state of metamorphosis—the result of centuries of allowing others to construct our image. For years we were depicted as fools, barely able to walk and hold a conversation simultaneously. We were made savage, almost non-human, with a brutal side that undermined our ability to maintain control. Black women had two roles: the promiscuous seducer who threatened the order of society or the overweight matriarch who controlled the family, especially their weak and docile husbands. The impact of the movie *Birth of a Nation*, which predicted the consequences of the South losing the Civil War, made Black male sexuality out to be feared. He was a dangerous creature with a low moral capacity -never to be trusted around white women.

The twentieth century was all about reconstructing the image of Black folk. It was a time to control how we were seen and described. Music, arts, dance, and poetry flourished during the Harlem Renaissance. The 50s and 60s saw Black-owned businesses and entrepreneurship enter the equation. The Civil Rights Movement unified us even more and fueled our desire to be viewed with respect. When we went out of the house, we made sure that we were presentable because we were representing ourselves, our families, and our communities.

The Black power movement asserted that we were strong in every way. Afros and African garb hinted at comfort in our skin, while television shows like *The Jeffersons* offered proof of our upward mobility. George, the successful cleaners' proprietor, made it to the big high-rise apartment in the sky. With him was his beautiful wife, Louise, and their ambitious and socially conscious son, Lionel, who felt comfortable putting white people in their place when they got out of line. When *The Cosby Show* became the number one watched show in the country, a blueprint for how we as Black folk truly wanted to be seen had arrived. Cliff, the doctor, with his attractive wife, who just so happened to be a brilliant lawyer, raised their kids in harmony, ensuring nurturing, discipline, and love always.

In the 90s and early part of the 21st century, Hollywood got on board, throwing money at films featuring African-Americans in a more positive light. There was *Soul Food, Love Jones, The Best Man,* and *Why Did I Get Married* for every *Boyz in The Hood, Juice,* and *Menace to Society* that described the state of emergency for young urban Black boys. Black folk received roles and scripts having storylines previously reserved in film for white people.

Our community's argument that there were no positive images of Black people had disappeared. We had Oprah and President Obama for our children. And so many more.

Black folk understand the importance of image and how this impacts their ability to get a job, their relationships with neighbors, and their challenge in directing their children. They go to great lengths to hold themselves accountable for their role in helping to create positive images of Black people by countering negative ones whenever possible. Black folk frown and become insulted when others belittle their worth and view them as one-dimensional.

Because the stereotype is that Black folk are always angry, They are sure to greet those they pass on the sidewalk by smiling and saying "good morning" or "hey" to neighbors. Black folk love to converse with people, ensuring that others understand how well versed they are. Black folk easily engage on topics of politics and world affairs. Debates about sports, entertainment, education, and religion all come naturally to them. At work, they make sure that what they do is thorough. Black folk destroy any idea of inherent laziness, challenge the concept of "CP Time" and stress that they desire to improve the work environment for the next Black person who may come to work at that location.

Black Folk work hard to beautify their communities, organizing town watch groups, planting gardens in vacant lots, and painting over graffiti as often as it goes up. They know that the pride one takes in his neighborhood directly impacts how people feel about themselves. Black folk may not have the money to build a fancy fence around their home or even replace tired and worn windows, but they make sure that the property is clean of trash, debris, and anything else that may be considered an eyesore to neighbors.

Black folk will not financially support any organization, group, or person bent on doing irreversible harm to their image. For example, suppose a television station continuously promotes programs that place Black people in roles that reinforce stereotypes of the "Sambo," shiftless idiot, angry female, gangster, or ho. In that case, Black folk will boycott that channel. Likewise, entertainers who glorify violence, use sexually explicit lyrics, and promote ignorance over intelligence, violence over peace, division over unity or hate over love will also be banned. Not one cent of Black folk's hard-earned money will go to anything destructive to their image or their community.

What's Hard: media controlled images, Black folk celebrating negativity, "Me" over "We" mentality, stereotypical boxes

What's Cool: showing inter-cultural diversity, presenting Black folk as dynamic, positive mirrors for Black children

Author's Note: Just as cable television and the need to fill airtime with programming increased the number of Black representation available, streaming platforms have taken this to another level. Now, young directors and producers of color authenticate how Black folk are seen and, more importantly, expand and normalize the types of characters portrayed and stories told. Unfortunately, Black men get featured on local news in disheartening ways. Images of Black men committing unthinkable acts of violence are impossible to ignore. These images of Black folk create fear and resentment for many white people. Also, these images and violent acts make all Black folk guilty by pigmentation association. Although lumping people together and discriminating based on race is lazy, the consequence continues to be fewer opportunities for all Black folk regardless of how they live their lives.

ATTITUDE

"Ours is not the struggle of one day, one week, or one year. Ours is not the struggle of one judicial appointment or presidential term. Ours is the struggle of a lifetime, or maybe even many lifetimes, and each one of us in every generation must do our part." — John Lewis

&

"In all things that are purely social we can be as separate as the fingers, yet one as the hand in all things essential to mutual progress." — Booker T. Washington

CHAPTER 9

◆

ATTITUDE

One of my favorite motivational songs by the late Tupac Shakur is *Keep Your Head Up,* in which he alludes to the many problems that a person may have in life and the need for that person to persevere. But how can Black folk keep their heads up when many have to play the terrible hand they receive in the game of life? Not all of us come from middle-class families with two loving parents in the home. We are not all born in safe and nurturing communities. Not all of us can afford a private school education with numerous resources to assure academic success. Indeed, not all of us can claim to be from families devoid of drug or sexual abuse or serious medical issues. So goes the vicissitudes of life for most people, a series of good and bad episodes that shape how we view ourselves, the people around us, and the world.

How you handle the difficulties you face in life tells a lot about you. Some have the uncanny ability to bounce back from disappointments quickly, barely skipping a beat, while others stagger for a while, needing help from those that love them to stand up straight again. Others become floored by the unfortunate events in their lives, lack inner strength and a support group, and never recover.

Too many underestimate the gifts that come from positive thinking. As a result, they never benefit from the power and energy that comes from approaching each new day as if it is full of possibilities. Fortunately, the history of Black folk in this country tells a story of men and women with incredible tenacity and hopefulness. Enslaved for hundreds of years, denied fundamental human rights for nearly a century more, we found a way to stand up every time knocked down. Even when dealing with the unjust arm of the law, hanged and burned by the hands of racism and bigotry, or jailed by those attempting to deny civil liberties, Black folk's attitude towards persevering and the resolve to survive is unmatched in the history of the world.

Black folk establish early in life that things are not fair. As a result, they condition and prepare themselves accordingly. They become tough mentally, and they bounce back from the disappointments that strike them at work or home. In the face of death, racism, financial woes, depression, divorce or separation, crime, and health problems, Black folk find comfort that the setback will not defeat them. Black folk stand on the shoulders of people who undoubtedly had to face worse circumstances and survived. They believe that they will survive too and eventually prosper through prayer, dedication, friendship, family, and love.

This attitude drives Black folk to such high achievements in life. The racist supervisor at work prohibits them from receiving a promotion, having to work two jobs to support the family, or taking in a nephew or niece who may have momentarily lost his or her way; Black folk believe that they are problem solvers. Therefore, they organize a plan of action that allows them to overcome any barrier that prohibits their ability to move forward. The plan includes going back to school if knowledge is the limiting factor. They seek counseling or spiritual guidance for relationship or addiction issues. They organize committees and outreach programs to transform their community into thriving and nurturing environments for children. They spend quality time with their kids when they seem to be traveling down the wrong path—and replace negative people from their close circle with those who bring the type of positive energy that will allow them to rise.

Black Folk have the attitude that there is nothing they can not accomplish, which allows them to continue to break down all types of institutional barriers. They believe that they can not rely on others to fix that which harms the community, even as they continue to hold the government and others accountable for actions, laws, and practices that limit or hinder them. Moreover, Black folk accept the challenges laid out by those who have come before them. They realize they must be determined to leave the world a better place for their children.

What's Hard: instant gratification, lack of resilience, believing that you are owed something, attraction to negativity

What's Cool: can do mentality, builds self-confidence, belief that I can make the difference, failure not an option, belief that success awaits me

RESPECT

"In recognizing the humanity of our fellow beings, we pay ourselves the highest tribute." — Thurgood Marshall

&

"My humanity is bound up in yours, for we can only be human together." — Desmond Tutu

CHAPTER 10

———◆———

RESPECT

When Aretha Franklin belted out the song *Respect*, the Black community, and America for that matter, had lots of fun constructing a definition of the word. Women wanted the same respect as men, demanding equality in the workplace and the home. In return, men wanted more respect from women as they felt the playing field becoming more level. They wanted to take a closer look at gender roles and became more biblical about arguing about a man's place as the head of the household. Black folk wanted white people to respect every nuance about them they felt was still misunderstood.

The problem was that no one could agree on precisely what respect meant. As a result, people felt disrespected over just about anything. But, if we are honest, we can agree on the definition of "respect." Deep in our souls, we know when we are respectful and when we are not, whether for ourselves or others. Does the man who yells out all types of obscenities to the scantily dressed girl walking down the street believe he is being respectful? Does that same little girl, with more of her butt cheeks revealed than covered, think she is showing herself respect? Throughout any given day, we face many opportunities to show respect to or disrespect ourselves and others. Would you consider your choice not to pick up the gum wrap you dropped on the ground in front of your neighbor's house respectful or disrespectful? How about your unpleasant and highly critical thoughts about the attractive person you never met, just because they enter the same room as you?

In the Black community, our struggles with the concept of respect play out in neighbor-to-neighbor confrontations, teenage pregnancy, destruction of property, and, importantly, the relationships between the elder and the younger generations. It is becoming increasingly more difficult for those men who are still willing and able to act as mentors and surrogate fathers in any given neighborhood because young Black boys, although wanting and deserving of love, do not know how to receive it. Gestures of assistance or a push in the right direction by another man signify disrespect.

This brainwashing results in disrespect towards the men who attempt to act as positive role models in the community. They are cursed, threatened, and even mocked for doing what is right. Is serving the community where you are living and raising your kids respectful? What feels disrespectful to these men, who work real jobs, take care of their families and still find time to help others, is that they are laughed at and labeled as weak when in reality, they are the most vital and most noble men we have to offer.

Respect is earned, and Black folk take this seriously when raising their kids, at work, in their relationships with others, and indeed themselves. They start with self-respect because they know it is difficult to respect others if they hold themselves in little regard. Thus, Black folk spend many years, and sometimes a lifetime, doing things they believe make themselves better. Actions as diverse as going back to school, quitting a job if their kids need them at home, going to work to provide more opportunities for their family, volunteering at an animal shelter, or joining the Big Brother or Big Sister Programs all garner respect. Self-respect may come from planting a tree to replace the one you cut down or making it to every parent-teacher conference while your kids are in grade school. Respect for Black folk may be losing the 10-15 pounds that allow extra years to spoil grandchildren, giving up smoking or drinking, praying more often, organizing block clean-up days, and special activities for the kids.

By starting with good feelings about themselves, Black folk can go out and positively influence the people around them. Because Black folk respect themselves, they hold themselves responsible for their interactions with others. For example, they do not look down on their neighbor who may have fallen on hard times; they offer to help to get her back on the right path. In addition, Black folk find ways to deal with disagreements without becoming violent; fighting in the street while their children watch from the porch would not be respectful.

Black folk teach their kids that with age comes a certain level of respect and that they should act accordingly in the presence of an adult. If they have a problem with an adult, they should immediately tell their parents and allow them to say what needs to be said. Children of Black folk know that experimenting with illegal drugs, abusing alcohol, and having unprotected sex are all ways to disrespect their bodies. Girls learn that allowing a man to manipulate them mentally or physically is also a disrespect to themselves. At school, teachers and the education process are in high regard. Black folk respect the power of information and its life-changing qualities. They are respectful of history and understand the struggles that come when chasing opportunity.

What's Hard: failing to give grace, disrespect leading to violence or death, lack of self-respect

What's Cool: self-respect feeding mind, body, and spirit, promoting care or neighbors and community

AMBITION

"Never be limited by other people's limited imaginations."
— Dr. Mae Jemison

&

"I am lucky that whatever fear I have inside me, my desire
to win is always stronger." — Serena Williams

CHAPTER 11

AMBITION

When Black folk tell their kids that they can be anything in the world if they work hard enough, are they truthful? Indeed, the first Black president in the history of this country gave greater credence to this statement. In the past, these words spoken by parents and teachers seemed more cliché than anything, with children understanding that the point was for them to work hard to be successful at something. But there were always hints of limitations, even warnings that there would be people who would purposefully stand in their way. People that did not want them to succeed.

I do not believe that any logical person would dare argue against the fact that Black folk are the descendants of some of the most ambitious people ever to walk the face of the earth. Look at how far we have come since the Emancipation Proclamation. In this country, Black folk have always aspired to bring real and substantial change to the destructive ways of thinking that have permeated people's minds for generations. Even when books had to be hidden under floor planks to keep from being discovered, those enslaved dreamed and aspired for things that could change their lives. Despite having no skills, no money, and no education, they devised plans to survive and prosper, gaining what information they could along the way. A key element to this salvation was ambition.

Now we have examples of the power of ambition all around us. Black doctors, lawyers, teachers, writers, politicians, and entertainers discuss how they chased their dreams. Black children need not look far for stories of ambition and achievement; they are but a few clicks away on the computer.

However, our children may not seek these examples on their own and must often be guided to them by parents. Black parents should also provide their children with examples from their community of people who, with ambition, can do good for themselves and those around them.

Thoughts of the past drive Black folk and are used as motivation to do well in the present and future. They store away all the condescending comments from those that claimed we were not smart enough, disciplined enough, or mentally strong enough to do more than clean up after white folk. It is not hard for Black folk to find motivation for their ambitions, for they know that if they make it, they will be able to take more Black people along with them. Their ambition is often driven by others' hate but fueled by the support and encouragement of the people around them.

Content with their accomplishments but never satisfied, Black folk constantly aim to provide a better life for their children. They challenge their offspring to accomplish more than they have been able to and foster an environment of achievement that spans generations. Black folk strive to produce exceptional work, for they want promotion when it becomes available. They teach their children the importance of writing down their goals and the significance of sharing their dreams with people that may be able to support them. It would not be unusual to enter the home of Black folk and notice that they have created a board with the goals of every family member written on it for daily reference. If a child wants to achieve A's on every Algebra test this year, the parent can help by providing the necessary support. They may ask, "Do you really want to spend another half hour on TikTok, or would you rather spend that time going over the order of operations for the test on Friday morning?"

Since ambition comes naturally to Black folk, they constantly look for new and exciting challenges. These things may include starting their own business, going back to school, attempting to earn the mastery of a new skill or foreign language, or, most importantly, finding positive ways to touch the lives of others. They aim to save as many Black people as possible and live their lives, countering negative stereotypes whenever possible. If the stereotype is that they are loud, boisterous, and uncompromising, Black folk speak truth calmly, softly, and with great clarity. If the stereotype is that Black folk are lazy, they make sure to show up to work early and leave late. Whatever the stereotype may be, Black folk are motivated to debunk it if it is harmful. Doing so will hopefully provide the next generation of Black people with even more opportunities.

What's Hard: requires sacrifice, doubts of others, low self-esteem and expectations, self-fulfilling prophecy

What's Cool: creates resilience, fuel for dreams, provides internal and external goals, sparks entrepreneurial and community success

Author's Note: Ambition fuels achievement on personal and professional levels. When ambition gets paired with support and opportunity, Black folk move mountains. This is why it is vital to ignite the flame of ambition in all Black children. There are many motivational stories to share where the outcome of being ambitious has led to incredible success. For example, Michael Jordan credits his entire career to his ambition to be the greatest basketball player ever. To accomplish this, not only did he have a perhaps unmatched work ethic, his dream was fueled by the desire to prove others wrong or to punish them for doubting him. Also, consider Sean Combs and his story of sitting on his steps as a young child and watching his neighbors enjoy their family pool. He never got invited to join them, and this sparked his ambition to have more and to be able to provide for himself all that he desired. A short stay at Howard University honing his promotional skills, and later support by Andre Harrell, led to the mogul and businessman we know as Diddy.

PARENTING

"I love, love children. I love being a dad. It's one of the joys of life. In fact, you can take it all away from me tomorrow, but don't take away my children." — Idris Elba

&

"You are your best thing." — Toni Morrison

CHAPTER 12

PARENTING

To find arguably the number one culprit in the decline of the Black family, we need not look further than what has become an incredibly feeble way of parenting. Once, clear lines separated the parent from the child, but confusion entered the equation as time progressed, and many suggested that children deserved more rights. Parents opted for another approach to raising children: being seen as their equals and a friend. With this relationship renegotiation, children started believing they could speak, act and make decisions like adults. The matter compounded within the Black community as value changes coincided with the pilgrimage of Black men to anywhere outside the household. Very young women, who were not yet mature or stable enough to take care of themselves, were forced to shoulder the sole responsibility for families.

Parenting is an art form, if not a science, requiring far more of you than any task you can complete. However, if done correctly, the parents can become the deciding factor in providing a child with the best opportunity to find success. Parents must be seen as role models for their children, not relying on another person to do this job for them. Black parents must model the attributes of strength, compassion, and intelligence and demonstrate courage, wisdom, work ethic, and discipline.

Children learn from their parents their views on how to respect their partners, financial literacy, emotional and educational discipline, a sense of service and community, spirituality, and methods of communication. When parents think about this logically, why would we trust anyone else to teach these important lessons to those we love so much? Why would we relinquish this power?

For Black folk, parenting is a shared responsibility between adults. It does not matter if the two are not married, divorced, or separated. The duties required to nurture a child ready to face the challenges of this world require both to be present. To Black folk, there is no superior challenge, no greater joy, than to produce a healthy child in mind, body, and soul. They smile when they realize that it is because of their labor that their child has graduated from college, gives back to the community, and has the capacity and knowledge to raise healthy and productive kids of their own.

Black folk acknowledge that they should be the example they seek for their children, believing it unfair to hand this responsibility over to anyone else. So, if they want their children to work hard, they work hard, if they desire their children to be respectful, they show respect, if they strive to have kids who are generous, spiritual, and well read, then they make sure that these attributes represent who they are as parents as well. Black folk hold themselves to this type of accountability, so they do not come across as hypocritical or fake to their children.

While parenting, Black folk promote love over hate and forgiveness instead of holding grudges. They believe this reasoning is good food for the spirit and builds character in young people. They teach their children to value family, people, and community above material things and that they must always attempt to help those that require assistance.

Above all, for Black folk, parenting means being present, sacrificing some of their interest in favor of their children's passions. It means putting aside whatever issues may have surfaced between parents to satisfy the needs of the children. It also means showing up for athletic events, birthday parties, curriculum nights, play days, music recitals, or any time the child needs to talk. In these moments, Black folk build bonds, earn respect, boost confidence, and raise children.

What's Hard: children exposure to negative forces, busy schedules, complicated partner relationships, technology, setting boundaries, differentiating parenting from friendship, conditional love, discipline, single parent households

What's Cool: chance to positively influence that which you love, providing and protecting, modeling what you want them to do and be, celebrating children success and achievements

Author's Note: The role of parenting for Black folk has only increased in importance. Our communities have never needed parents to guide the choices and decisions of young Black children more. Many young Black folk find themselves in peril, requiring the love and care of parents to protect them from temptations and pressures that compromise their ability to make good choices and sacrifice any chance at success or a productive future. Consequently, the number of young Black children committing or being victims of violent and deadly crime is rising, and this stress on Black families and communities is not sustainable.

SPIRITUALITY

"Faith makes things possible, not easy." —Rosa Parks

&

"You really can change the world if you care enough."
— Marian Wright Edelman

CHAPTER 13

SPIRITUALITY

Black folk have always been spiritual. We credit spirituality for giving us the fortitude to survive the heinous tortures suffered while enslaved. In the 1960s, Dr. Martin Luther King's premise of nonviolence centered on the teachings of Mahatma Gandhi. Techniques he used for resistance required a heightened sense of spirituality. Dr. King preached that you should do what is right in the presence of what is wrong, meet hate with an abundance of love, and forgive those who harm you instead of seeking revenge against them. But spirituality is more than how we conduct ourselves towards other people. Spirituality is about our relationship with a higher being and how we choose to live our lives based on this relationship.

It does not matter to me how you identify religiously. You can claim to be Catholic, Methodist or Protestant, Jewish or Muslim, or practice Hinduism or Buddhism. What is important is how you live your life based on your chosen religious teachings. You may worship in a synagogue, a church, a hall, meetinghouse, mosque, or temple. What is important is how you live life once you leave the brick and mortar. You may read the Bible every morning, the Koran over lunch, and the Talmud before bed. What is important is how the words guide your actions throughout the day.

In the Black community, the church has lost its ability to reach those that need the most guidance. It was once the glue of the community, where business was conducted under God's watchful eyes. The church was the refuge for all those lost souls who had nowhere else to turn, the place that helped to raise political, spiritual, and socially conscious young Black children, and it promoted the purest ideals of humanity. But unfortunately, the church has relinquished this power over the people that walk past its doors daily. People no longer fear what may happen to them in the afterlife; they are too busy trying to find a way to survive today. Therefore, Black folk must once again harness the power of religion and spirituality to provide a protective cloak for those battling all types of figurative and literal demons.

Black folk must be grounded in their spirituality, using it to provide a framework for conducting actions with others and monitoring their own choices and behavior. Spirituality helps to remain humbled about success and honest with oneself and others about failures. If Black folk develop a strong sense of moral and ethical guidance through their spirituality, this will make serving and helping others a common occurrence. Moreover, these acts of kindness will not be extraordinary but expected, making it easy to pass on this message to Black children.

Although like everyone else, Black folk make mistakes and have lapses of judgment, because of their strong spirituality, they work to correct the wrongdoing and strive to mend relations that their actions may have harmed. These efforts require being able to admit to being wrong and the strength to ask for forgiveness. In return, Black folk's spirituality makes them forgive people as they understand that we are all flawed in many ways. Black folk make it a point to let people know that they are willing to help anyone willing to help themselves.

Spirituality's moral and ethical structure helps Black folk question their actions. For example, decisions concerning cheating on a partner or adultery become clearer. Thoughts of being part of some criminal act or putting yourself or your children in harm's way demand a different consideration. Even talking behind a friend's back, sabotaging a co-worker's attempt at promotion, not reporting a crime, or failing to protect the innocent and victimized become much clearer through spirituality.

What's Hard: keeping faith through life's disappointments, more people are atheist or agnostic, temptations and desire for instant gratification, less consensus on what is right or wrong and moral and immoral

What's Cool: level of moral and ethical accountability beyond self, provides pathway to forgive and for forgiveness, strengthens internal and external relationships, empowers places of worship to support people and communities

BLACK MEN

"The strongest, toughest men all have compassion. They're not heartless and cold. You have to be man enough to have compassion — to care about people and about your children. — Denzel Washington

&

"If you have no confidence in self, you are twice defeated in the race of life." — Marcus Garvey

CHAPTER 14

BLACK MEN

It isn't easy to know how Black men have gone astray or how we have become so divided despite sharing the type of past that usually fosters unity, togetherness, and a love and passion for those with a similar resemblance and affinity. Once a leader, provider, and protector in homes, Black men are often reduced to a sidekick, a person not even expected to be around. A significant name on a birth certificate but irrelevant for the remainder of his child's life. The person that causes more harm than good and creates more problems than he can solve.

Despite cries for help from Black women and children alike, many Black men seem unable or unwilling at times to do what is necessary to regain their proper standing in the home, the community, and society. Are we not ready to be honest about the mess that we have created? Are we not angry, embarrassed, or disgusted enough at what has transpired? The truth is that not until we admit to our wrongdoings can we right ourselves and work to establish the type of pride and respect that we desire and deserve.

We must teach our boys what it means to be tough. We must teach them that standing on a corner selling drugs, robbing innocent people of their money, burglary, assault, murder, and the pimping of women are all signs of weakness. They are all signs that we do not have the capacity, discipline, or heart to advance in life without cheating. That we are not tough enough to get up at 5:00 am every day to catch a bus to work to make an honest day's pay. That we are not resourceful enough to do without until we have earned enough to have what we desire. That we are not compassionate enough to stop ourselves from killing our brothers and sisters for material things or strong enough to be a father to the children that we create.

As Black men, we can no longer put on the charade that we are happy with ourselves. Could we be satisfied knowing that Black women surpass us economically, educationally, and in their ability to uplift our communities? Are we not ashamed of the number of brothers rotting away in prison cells and the thousands more who choose to drop out of high school every year? Are we not tired of watching the news or reading the newspapers and seeing our faces plastered next to descriptions of crimes that shake our souls? Haven't we had enough of portraying ourselves as gangsters, pimps, drug dealers, womanizers, and heartless idiots?

Every Black man must vow to change his life and the lives of those around him for the better. We must learn from our mistakes in the past and focus every ounce of energy that we can muster to ensure that these mistakes don't repeat. We must help those floating in a world of negativity, selling drugs or weapons. Black men committing crimes or already in prison must find some form of salvation. Those denying fatherhood or neglecting to support their kids must immediately do better. Black men making excuses to remain uneducated or failing to improve their skills must know that this life is not sustainable. Those terrorizing neighborhoods, destroying communities, and killing the hopes of a generation of young Black children must be held accountable.

The damage to our community has been substantial, but some actions can be forgiven if Black men are willing to change right now. But, this forgiveness will be the most difficult challenge of our lives because it will require each individual, that's every single Black man in this country, to take responsibility and be accountable for his actions.

Black men must wear the label of manhood as a badge of honor. They can't get fooled by the fakers who attempt to convince others that carrying a gun, killing our brothers and sisters, and acting like a thug makes them a man. Black men should be insulted by this, for they understand just how difficult it is, and how tough it can become, to provide for a family honestly. They know they are the strongest men living because they can achieve despite all the forces that stand in their way. They must even deal with other Black men bent on making this task difficult for them by behaving in a manner that makes all Black folk guilty by association.

Black men must do anything short of degrading and destroying their families' legacy to secure their children's future. If it means enduring the hateful words of an ex-wife or partner to remain active in their child's life, that is what they do. If it means taking a second or third job cleaning buildings to provide more opportunities to the people they love, that's what they do. If it means going back to school at night or improving a skill by volunteering somewhere, this is what they do to further themselves. If they have to start a neighborhood basketball or baseball team to help young kids to stay active and out of trouble, that is what they do.

Black men must summon their power and display it daily. It must be found in the confidence of their smiles as they make a presentation in front of the board at work or in the sleepy eyes of a father who just pulled a double shift to earn enough money to send his daughter to dance class. It must be found in their loving fingers when they turn off the television and in their words to explain to their children why they cannot allow them to watch Black folk behave in such ways. Finally, it must be found in their raised hand, the first to volunteer for the neighborhood town watch, and the shaking of their head while refusing illegal drugs or stolen goods.

Teachers must know that Black men will be the ones asking the difficult questions on parent night and the ones sitting in the front row for all of their child's school performances. Neighbors must know that Black men will greet them with kind words and respect their property. Employers will praise Black men for their work ethic and thoroughness, and co-workers will marvel at their drive and ambition.

Most importantly, Black men will define themselves in the most positive ways and never embrace anything that portrays them as one-dimensional. They will understand the complexity of who they are. They can enjoy books as much as they do sports, like jazz music, classical, and R&B, and look as cool in shorts and sneakers as they do in their dark business suits. Black men will show respect to their friends and the homeless brother down the street, speak slang and the King's English, like to party and praise the Lord in church, be strict and discipline their kids and allow them space and room to grow. Black men will even honor and respect their partners while establishing themselves as a leader in the home.

All of this is possible for Black men with self-respect and pride, keeping in mind that they are in charge of their own destiny. Black men, must believe that success comes to those who chase it with tunnel vision and to those with a plan to be disciplined and focused. They must expect the chase to be difficult, but embrace this challenge because they are tough. Black men will meet inevitable setbacks, disappointments, and failures with determination, more dedication, and greater resolve. They will view the obstacles in the race as their greatest motivational tools, loving to prove people wrong and reconfigure the perceptions of others.

What's Hard: number of Black men committing crimes or in prison, declining college graduation rates, being feared, lack or representation in STEM fields and schools, mental health, antagonistic or nonexistent relationship with co-parent

What's Cool: the impact of presence alone on academic outcomes for children, trend-setters, athletic and artistic achievements, fraternities, potential of untapped power and influence

Author's Note: I had a sobering moment recently as I decided to write down the names of childhood friends who have lost their lives to gun violence or are currently serving unimaginable years in prison. After reaching the 10th name, ten Black boys from the same two or three West Philadelphia blocks, I stopped, unable and unwilling to finish what I had started. The thought of adding even one more name, one more deceased or caged Black man, to the torn-out piece of paper was anxiety-provoking and more than I could handle.

The sad and horrifying truth is that my experience is not an anomaly. The lists are perhaps even longer for some Black folk that come from areas like I did, rich in poverty and disinvestment. Black men are dying at an alarming rate, and many more will meet a similar fate if significant change does not happen. Unfortunately, the solutions, if any, are elusive. The lack of education, poverty, and hopelessness that many experience, combined with the proliferation of drugs and guns in the community, exacerbate the challenges.

There are many Black men to celebrate, and we should honor them.

They navigate the most challenging and treacherous path to success than any demographic in this country. But it is difficult to find joy in the plight of Black men when watching or reading the news feels like they are describing an endangered species. I pray that in my lifetime, there are actionable solutions to what ails us, Black men, so that we too can find internal, brotherly, and communal peace.

BLACK WOMEN

"The only thing that separates women of color from anyone else is opportunity." — Viola Davis

&

"But what of Black women?… I most sincerely doubt if any other race of women could have brought its fineness up through so devilish a fire." — W. E. B. Du Bois

CHAPTER 15

BLACK WOMEN

Unlike any other race of people, Black folk have depended on the strength and backbone of women for survival. Every significant movement concerning Black people in this country became prosperous, even behind the scenes, from Black women's toil, energy, and support. Forced into the role of provider and protector, Black women have demonstrated an amazing ability to adapt and advance in society. Born a double minority, she has had to deal not only with racial barriers but gender obstacles as well.

Black women have constantly tried to battle the images of the overweight maid or the highly emotional and uncompromising friend. To this day, she struggles to find a balance between being the matriarch and being too dominant or aggressive. Yet, she has made substantial strides in all walks of life, competing at the most prestigious universities and advancing in the realms of business and politics. Also, she has somehow managed to be the only constant in the Black household.

Rightfully, Black women have become less threatening to the rest of society. Unlike their male counterparts, they are embraced in ways Black men have never experienced. Black women are seen as more powerful and equally intelligent as white women. Although it is racism that attributes masculinity to their extreme confidence, they have earned positive labels of being opinionated, assertive, and ready to lead. Black women's strength is unquestionable, and even criticisms about her hair and body type have proven to be minuscule obstacles to her mobility and attractiveness.

Black women are dynamic in many ways, able to juggle numerous responsibilities seamlessly. They are as comfortable creating deals on Wall Street as they are in making a happy home, and they raise their children to be productive members of society. These women have figured out ways to maneuver through the system enough so that it does not deny them of anything they cherish. In addition, they understand that others will challenge them, which incentivizes them to prepare continuously.

Able to compete at all levels and in every field, Black women do so with pride, intelligence, and eloquence. Although they are often only one of a few at their places of business, they approach every work assignment confidently and never allow numbers to hinder opportunities for advancement. Black women are successful on all fronts, be it the workplace, the household, sorority life, or the community.

They are sure to teach their children to value their bodies and to respect their family. In addition, they work to secure healthy relations with partners that advance them spiritually, emotionally, and educationally.

Black women are often teachers, having to educate others at work and socially about cultural differences we have as Black folk. Never looking for acceptance but often willing to help others to better their understanding, Black women develop modes of communication that allow them to be effective in various settings. Because they are socially conscious, they aim to debunk stereotypes of Black women as full of attitude and boisterous. If only to make it easier for her sisters, Black women counter all stereotypes to show our diversity as a people.

Not willing to settle for less than they deserve, Black women attract partners who demonstrate tremendous ambition and a love of self. They understand and appreciate how difficult it is to be a Black man, but they are not attracted to those who cheat or quit at this challenge. They will not allow negative influences around their children nor submit to a partner aiming to destroy their self-confidence or worth. Instead, Black women are attracted to partners who uplift Black folk and those that can teach their children how to love themselves and community.

Above all, some Black women are mothers, and raising well-adjusted children is a priority. They are loving, supportive, nurturing, and honest with their children, helping them to understand that it is their job to protect them from vices and things that may limit them. If this means telling their children "No" at times and setting limits to what is and is not acceptable behavior, they do so because their love requires that they do. Black women understand that they must make moral and ethical decisions for their children until they can make these decisions for themselves.

What's Hard: single-parent households, pay and health care discrepancies, sexual harrassment and abuse, intersection of being Black and female

What's Cool: level of academic and professional achievement, redefining standards of beauty, entrepreneurship, sororities, Kamala Harris

FINAL THOUGHTS

"I will not take 'but' for an answer." – Langston Hughes

&

"I am no longer accepting the things I cannot change. I am changing the things I cannot accept."
— Angela Y. Davis

&

"Change will not come if we wait for some other person or some other time. We are the ones we've been waiting for. We are the change that we seek."
— Barack Obama

FINAL THOUGHTS

My final thoughts intentionally and deservingly go to Black boys. I have three of them myself, and as the late Marvin Gaye offered, "Ain't *no mountain high enough, Ain't no valley low enough, Ain't no river wide enough to keep me from you.*"

Dear Black Boys,

You are amazing! I know you may not hear these words as often as you should but please never doubt this. You are amazing. And because you are amazing I watch you do things that no other humans on this planet are capable of doing. You have to juggle school, sometimes work, and occasionally unbelievable responsibilities in the home– and you have to do so without complaining or demonstrating any sign of weakness. You are told, and you have accepted, that showing pain is weakness, and because of this, your exterior may come across as hard and cold when you are gentle and kind. I see this kindness in you. I see your intelligence, talents, gifts, and ability to lead. If you weren't so amazing it might be more difficult to see these things. But I see them clearly. Amazing can't be hidden.

Amazing Black boys, you have amazing Black men to look up to when needed. And whereas we are not as amazing as you, we have provided examples of doctors, lawyers, civil rights activists, teachers, writers, athletes, entertainers, spiritual leaders, fathers, uncles, and brothers to guide you. You will need these resources for some important work that awaits you.

No need to worry about this important work because I think you are so amazing that you hold the answers to some pretty difficult questions inside. Some of these questions impact the entire Black community. Others are more difficult to answer than any question on any test you will ever take. Questions like how do we save all of our brothers from pathways that lead to prison, or worse yet, violent death? Questions like how do we unlock the doors to quality education and prosperity for all of us? Questions such as how do we love ourselves and those around us just as much? Even questions about how to reclaim and restore Black men's harm to our communities

Although you are amazing, some people do not acknowledge this. They can only see your scars and your fears and the sides of you that you too dislike. Some are even rooting for you to fail. For your amazing to be extinguished or locked away in a cell forever. But you will never let this happen. You are too proud of your amazingness not to protect and defend it. Too smart not to grow and share it.

As a Black man, I am unapologetically biased– but I honestly believe that no other group is amazing enough to do what you must do. So actualize your amazing, and collectively, Black boys, the world as you know it, as we know it, will never be the same.

Warmly,
Keino

EXPLORING RACE & SCHOOLS

Through my writing, I have explored the concept of race for most of my adult life. Some of this writing has been personal and some professional. Other writings have been expressions of my racial journey and unpacking Blackness through poetry and fiction. These writings have proven therapeutic and have demanded deep and honest reflection. Mainly, I have considered how race impacts my life and the lives of those like me. I have also pondered my positionality in spaces where being Black has been both a nest and a cage. My writings consistently intend to further my understanding of self and provide a window to my racialized experience for others. The following is a small sample of this work focused on race and schools.

DECOUPLING FROM RACIAL PRESSURES LEGITIMIZES ORGANIZATIONS

Abstract

Institutional theory works to understand and identify social relationships within an organization and to consider how stability or changes to norms and patterns in structure impact both internal and external perceptions and reality. Through institutional theory, reflections on rationalized thinking, formal and informal structures that legitimate practices, and how an organization responds to environmental pressures and turbulence is considered. It provides the appropriate theoretical framework for examining the school organization in this paper. It offers insight into how school personnel decouples from standard practices when the environmental pressure deals specifically with race and why doing so reinforces institutional code that protects the school from more severe external turbulence.

Introduction

Fox Academy is an independent Quaker institution established in 1838. Grounded in rich tradition and guided by stewardship, peace, integrity, community, equality, and simplicity, the school has often found itself ahead of the social benchmarks surrounding diversity issues. For example, the first African American student enrolled in 1938. Although this is 60 years after the end of the Reconstruction Era, in the United States, Jim Crow Laws dominated the voice and practice around race, solidifying segregation until the Brown vs. Board of Education decision in 1954. Today, Fox Academy and other Quaker institutions struggle to reconcile why they were so slow in desegregating their schools. Yet, those independent schools desegregated earlier enjoy more legitimacy around the principle of equality.

Since the twentieth century, Fox Academy has been steadfast in exploring other forms of diversity, understanding the complications and inconsistencies with messaging that were sure to surface around the concept of tuition and elitism. This struggle is as real in the pinnings of the institution now as at any time in the school's tenure. Tuition prices, marketing strategies, and competition often compromise the mission and vision of the school. These environmental pressures have impacted how the school deals with conflicts involving the concept of race, departing from standard practices of conflict resolution and engaging with racial problems in ways that are inconsistent with how challenges around other forms of difference get resolved. This paper will examine how Fox Academy responds differently when the turbulence or environmental pressure is couched by the concept of race and explore why this happens.

The answers gained by this inquiry may prove vital in two ways. First, if Fox Academy responds to pressures that deal specifically with race differently than other pressures around forms of difference, can organizational value or cost be measured from this? Secondly, does dealing with the concept of race in a way that isolates it from how other forms of difference get managed impact the legitimacy of all conflict resolution protocols in the organization? Indeed, the answers to these questions produce myriad pathways to explore further, but they may also go beyond the perimeters of this paper. Consequently, they get noted in the conclusion section.

Finally, as the definition of diversity has proven fluid and robust in educational settings, with race, gender, and religion joined by age, socioeconomic status, physical and learning differences, geographic location, and even opinions and ways of thinking, the scope of this inquiry will consider organizational responses to pressures around the social construction of race in comparison to environmental stresses (other local organizations) brought on by the management of gender nonconforming students and that of academic competition. The two were selected because they demonstrate significant organizational differences in how they get managed in relation to race pressures. They also offer some interesting insight about institutionalized learning. Organizations store knowledge, and this learning reinforces procedures, norms, and rules that create social context (March, 1991).

Organizational Learning

Exploration and exploitation processes can work in opposition or in tandem with one another in organizational learning (March, 1991). At Fox Academy, they often compete for organizational resources, forcing the school to make intentional and thoughtful choices between the two. Exploration involves new possibilities, and exploitation relies on the stability of old certainties (Winter 1971; Levinthal and March, 1981). Their differences in regard to how organizations operate can be looked at in terms of how much risk and the possibility of reward are associated with each (March, 1991).

Over the last two years, Fox Academy has invested tremendous financial and personnel resources to explore maker space technology, ideology, and pedagogy. This exploration of this decade's "STEM" education directly responds to what the private school market demands, as competition from neighboring schools fosters a level of isomorphism in the name of legitimacy. Organizations often compete in this market, as positionality can establish them as a leader and innovative or as a follower and behind in educational pedagogy (March, 1991). Timing dramatically influences an organization's choice to utilize either exploration or exploitation.

As exploration involves experimentation and risk-taking, along with greater flexibility, the institution is bracing for feedback concerning the programming. It eagerly awaits measurables as evidence that the new practices around educating children will translate into dollars. This rational approach, as explained by both Taylor (1911) and Weber (1949) is heavy in organizational goal specificity, with administrators, in this case, engaging in approaches aimed at efficiency. Decisions about the Maker Space were hierarchical and through committee appointment, as opposed to individual volunteerism and faculty voice.

A similar exploration has occurred almost simultaneously as the very public, step-by-step conceptualizing of the Maker Space. With considerable economic and personnel power, Fox Academy grappled with a changing student and parent population, specifically those identifying as gender fluid or gender nonconforming. Again, like in the building of the Maker Space, the school consistently responded to the environmental pressure. The chart below demonstrates Fox Academy's response to both pressures, focusing on the clarity of the steps taken and the commitment to exploration to address the stress.

Table 1: Steps followed to address environmental pressures of makerspace facility and curriculum and gender non-conforming initiatives.

Initiative	Environmental Pressure	Funding	Committee Work	Communication	Result of Pressure
Maker Space	Competition Isomorphism Tution	Capital Campaign	2yrs Internal/ External Members Consultants Bids	Letters to faculty, parents, Alum, media 6 information Sessions	New Maker Space Director of Programming
Gender Nonconforming	Same Gender Parents Nonconforming students and faculty	Private Donors Board of Trustees	1yr Internal/ External Members Paid Consultants	Letters to faculty/parents Alum 3 Information Sessions for Parents/Faculty Evening Community Event	Non-gendered Bathrooms in Every Building 3 PD days for faculty training 2Non-gendered Locker Rooms Removal of some gender specific language from publications

Although the Maker Space does not meet the standard of a form of "diversity," it provides organizational insight concerning the use of exploration in response to environmental pressure. The school engaged in learning, looking outward in ways that impact practice.

But, most importantly, the school's response to the pressure, even with all the uncertainty around implementation, is intentional and informed.

In both situations, it is important to acknowledge that the response to the pressure offers the possibility of value in the end for the organization. In the case of the Maker Space, not only does the school present itself as both innovative and in step with trending educational practice, the benefit to students is evident, as experimentation, collaboration, and pragmatism are hallmarks of Dewey (1916). As for the implementation of the gender nonconforming initiatives, the school may certainly capitalize in the form of tuition dollars, as this innovative pivoting will be attractive to members of the LGBTQ communities (NAIS, 2016). This demographic is wealthier and more likely to have their children enroll in private school education.

March (1991) would suggest that organizations respond differently to adaptive processes or pressures that require sustained levels of exploration. Although the Maker Space initially demonstrated a method of exploration, the organization also had a clear goal. The same holds regarding gender-fluid initiatives, as this shared goal provided the institution with less uncertainty and more precise direction. In addition, the clarity of the organizational goals reinforces the organizational code regarding the importance of the initiatives and the organization's well-being.

Despite some teachers lacking congruence with the new initiatives around gender nonconformity practices that were to be implemented, due to the recommendations of the gender-neutral task force and the social capital of the members making up the committee, environmental pressures to conform were evident (Coborn, 2004). For example, one teacher expressed public displeasure that a faculty-only bathroom had been converted into a gender-neutral facility. Later that teacher spoke at a meeting for worship about why all community members needed to be open to reform around the issue. In digging deeper here, it was revealed that her Department Chair had reached out to her personally to improve her comfort level with the new practices. Likewise, administrators trained novice teachers to enhance competency and change behavior. Also, accountability was measurable in the language used to correspond with students and parents, the physical structures of the bathrooms, and the public correcting of both teachers and students when they engaged in language inconsistent with the new initiatives. These changes included using specific pronouns, removing words that grouped people by gender, i.e., "guys," and failing to ask students their preferred pronoun.

What is important to note is the lack of taken-for-grantedness associated with the innovation around gender nonconforming practices. Consider that there were clear measures for the initiatives that were public and private, and accountability was achieved as all written correspondence sent out was vetted by administrators. Most importantly, Fox Academy could leverage the school's Quaker history around issues of diversity, using clear messages to direct ties to the mission and vision of the school.

Even with this intentional and rational approach to addressing the environmental pressure, loose coupling was identified through the continuance of gender-specific sports teams, awards, and dress codes for the graduation ceremony. This type of loose coupling happens at the subunit level, as what is being said by the organization as a whole around gender nonconforming equity is not practiced in smaller school departments such as the athletic department (Pfeffer and Salanick, 1978).

Race as the Environmental Pressure

Fox Academy consistently responds to the pressures associated with gender nonconforming initiatives and those generated by academic competition. However, the organization breaks from this rational approach to decision-making when initiatives about race become the pressure, demonstrating less willingness to engage in exploration while utilizing sensemaking, decoupling, and ceremonial tactics to maintain legitimacy. Moreover, the organization relies more heavily on internal expertise and supporting code that allows novice teachers with little racial competency to remain isolated from accountability measures.

In the fall of 2016, the Fox Academy implemented an innovation to increase racial competence levels in the classroom. As part of the initiative, a movie was shown to all students and faculty-- shifting how race was to be covered in the classrooms, looking at the systems that support racism, and offering new vocabulary to be embraced during conversations about race with students, parents, and faculty. This new vocabulary, along with the changes to the curriculum, was to impact students of every grade and assist teachers in reevaluating their respective courses for racially insensitive material, images, and descriptions. As part of the initiative, teachers were to do in the following:

- Use the movie curriculum to engage in 5 different conversations with students about race
- Identify in their curriculum, language, material, and descriptions that are racially insensitive
- Select a reading from a list of books provided and attend the discussion groups about the text
- Engage in divisional follow-up discussions about the movie

According to Meyer and Rowan (1979), institutionalization happens when obligations and actualities create rules around social thought. The institution of race fits this definition. Race impacts how some are viewed and what is perceived as truth, and what is considered rational in dealing with the concept in an organizational setting. Moreover, Tolbert and McLaughlin (1994) suggest that the idea of teacher agency and autonomy, in response to specific environmental pressures, are the direct result of their professional communities, providing insight into how practices around racial pressures become code at Fox Academy.

When race becomes the environmental pressure, the code permits for faculty to decouple from previous protocol around difference in the organization, as goal ambiguity supports the agency and autonomy of teachers. Blau, (1970) places great emphasis on managing the many relationships of an organization. There are clear and rational ways for this to be done. He emphasizes a more significant emotional presence in understanding how organizations work, suggesting that when individual and organizational goals are inconsistent, the organization is far from rational. The challenge around racial pressures on an organization is that technical validation is difficult.

Consequently, Fox Academy's work around racial pressures resembles what Goffman (1967) describes as the logic of confidence and good faith. Fox Academy's very public showing of the movie, its invitation to the other Quaker schools to participate, and the question and answer session with the director of the film created legitimacy with institutionalized organizations, internal faculty members, and students. However, in practice, the school decoupled from the committee work, curriculum, and professional development training to navigate other pressures around difference (gender nonconforming) and academic competition (Maker Space).

This maintenance of face within Fox Academy buffers it from the uncertainty of the changing climate around race, while preserving and maintaining the appearance of a formal structure (March & Simon, 1958). Through goal ambiguity, compared to what got shared around gender nonconforming student initiatives and the Maker Space, there was no way to measure the effectiveness of practices asked of faculty around racial initiatives or of a rational way of measuring them. Thus, the use of good faith as it relates to the organizational pressure of race was useful in that it helped the faculty to assume that everyone was following the curriculum as assigned. Furthermore, there were no inspections that could produce data of noncompliance. This allowed for the benefits that come with ceremonial standards of worth to be still reaped by the organization. The latter legitimates the organization with both internal and external participants, presenting the organization as both healthy and rational.

Table 2 compares observed classroom behaviors of teachers concerning directives given for initiatives around race and gender nonconformity. They are examined through two lenses offered by Orton and Weick (1991). The first is the causation-seeking voice that looks at why some subunits become loosely coupled and have three elements of causal indeterminacy, fragmentation of external environment, and the one best suited for this paper, the fragmentation of internal environment. Similarly to what Lipsky (1993) suggested, street level bureaucrats, (teachers) work in ways that decouple when assigned goals and practices that are inconsistent.

The other lens is the direct effect-seeking voice that considers how loose- coupling around specific internal pressures in an organization is effective as a managerial tool (Orton & Weick, 1991). This voice also has three elements, including modularity, requisite variety, and the one used here, discretion. At Fox Academy, discretion plays out in the level of autonomy for teachers around the initiative. (Orton & Weick, 1991).

Observed Responses to Institutional Pressures Around Race & Gender Nonconforming Initiatives

Table 2: Table 2 shows the different responses by teachers based on congruence (Coburn, 2004) when race and gender nonconformity was the environmental pressure and given specific directives by administration.

Types of Responses	Definition	Race Responses	GN Responses	Level of Autonomy
Rejection	The teacher has little if any congruence with the institutional pressure as it does not make sense to them pedagogically (Does not implement practice)	Teacher does not engage in conversation with students about race at the conclusion of the program	Not observed in the classroom- All teachers engaged in conversation about language	Race: (High) Gender Nonconforming: (Low)
Decoupling/ Symbolic Response	Inferring the acceptance of a practice but not actually engaging in the practice	Teacher hands out the discussion questions after program but never engages the students in conversation	Teacher engaged in learning about the new initiatives through discussion questions but pronoun usage loosely-decoupled	Race (High) Gender Nonconforming (Moderate)
Parallel Structures	Finding balance between new practice and old ways of doing things. Teacher may gain an appreciation of the pedagogical value of the parallel practice	Teacher uses the guiding discussion questions for the program but adds several others that are intended to move to students in a direction more consistent with their beliefs	Teacher uses guiding questions in discussion but demonstrates sensemaking in connecting initiatives in ways that are not accurate	Race: (High) Gender Nonconforming: (High)

Assimilation	Understanding changes to instructional routines but not from a pedagogical viewpoint. Consequently, practice is not offered as intended--only in existing teacher schemes	Teaching uses the guiding questions but provides examples that misses the point of the programming and leads the class to a different focus	Not Observed	Race: (High) Gender Nonconforming (Low)
Accommodation	Teacher changes existing pedagogical assumptions and practices in favor of newly implemented practices; Teacher finds great value in new practice	Not Observed	Teacher engages in a full program including language of pronouns daily. Teacher discusses openly how her views have changed and how she sees her classroom space differently	Race: (High) Gender Nonconforming (High)

Understanding the Organization
Institutional Theory, Congruence & Sensemaking

Institutional theory helps explain the tension between conformity and efficiency by offering that many structures that promote conformity in the name of legitimacy often work against or fail to consider efficiency (Coborn, 2004). Although this is not always the case, more often than not, environmental pressures around race at Fox Academy sacrifice efficiency (getting things done with clear goals), conforming to old survival practices while maintaining legitimacy in the eyes of many. Institutional theory attempts to clarify the idea that some environmental pressures for conformity are efficiency-driven, but the overall belief is that it is difficult to conform and demonstrate technical efficiency (Rowan & Miskel, 1999).

The idea behind sensemaking is that people (teachers) reconceptualize messages, reframing them to accord with existing beliefs, codes and current practices. Thus, when new institutional pressures are placed on them to alter current practices, they engage in ways that allow their respective lenses to make the new information "make sense" to them (Coburn, 2004).

When congruence is low, as it often is with racial initiatives, teachers tend to reject the institutional pressure and change the practice in the classroom. If they do not entirely reject the new practice, they assimilate it into already existing views--but do not understand the practice on a pedagogical level. An example of this is when a faculty member who is part of the English Department taught the novel *The Adventures of Huckleberry Finn* despite it being contrary to the new racial initiative. Although the school enjoyed ceremonial legitimacy from the public denouncing of the text under the new racially sensitive practices, the reality was that the English Department split on the removal of the book. Thus, teacher autonomy and congruence with the initiative became a prevailing theme (Coburn, 2004).

Understanding the Organization

Central Questions: What prohibits the organization from responding to environmental pressures at the classroom and administrative levels? How do organizational routines support nonconformity of specific environmental stresses while others impact organizational practice?

Inertial pressures are those factors present in an organization that limit the impact of the environment on the organization itself. This resistance to change can be explained in the structures of an organization, some of which may be more significantly impacted by the environment while others are not (Hannan & Freeman, 1984). Organizations have higher structural inertia when environmental changes occur faster than an organization's ability to respond to such changes. Thus, the organization stays the same, and eventually, the environmental problem changes. Other factors that produce high levels of structural inertia include the age of the organization, size, and reproducibility. These factors are viewed as reliable and accountable. March (1991) suggests that environmental factors constantly change or influence organization structure and even practice, but that the organizations do not admit to this. This socializing towards the code allows members of an organization to say that one thing is happening when adjustments to described practices in response to environmental factors are always constant and more the reality (Hannan & Freeman, 1984).

In the Fox Academy environment, there is a high level of inertial pressure regarding race. This was costant even amid tremendous societal turbulence during the last year in the form of the Black Lives Matter Movement and a political campaign drenched in bigoted ideology. Despite both national events creating significant tremors beyond the confines of campus, Fox Academy was able to shield itself from the type of involvement tethered to the mission and vision of the school. Unlike the letters offered in full-throated support of needed changes to deal with the challenges of gender nonconformity, or the thoughtful and organized response to academic competition, the environmental pressures around race failed to produce a similar reaction.

Instead, Fox Academy partially resolved inconsistencies between ceremonial elements, and day-to-day activities, by maintaining organizational conformity and by cutting off external relations (no organized support efforts of BLM and no voice given to the harmful racial overtones of the presidential campaign on students) that would generate more significant turbulence. Instead, the organization promised reform.

The fixed state of promises of reform around race issues allows individuals critical of the present to believe in the organization's commitment to better. However, in response to environmental pressures around race, at Fox Academy, the practice and strategy offered to teachers and students are often devoid of time accountability. Phrases such as "we are considering" and "we are interested in hearing," as stated during student assemblies and faculty meetings, demonstrate care but lack the clarity and specificity of communications found around gender nonconformity issues. This strategy is effective as it makes the organization appear critical of itself and perhaps willing to try new things based on learning, collaboration, and even best practice (Meyer & Rowan, 1977).

Conclusion

At Fox Academy, when environmental pressures concerning race are present, examples of exploitation are easily discoverable. Whereas exploitation offers efficiency and refinement and consequences and feedback of practices are more expedient, the danger of exploitation is that organizations may ignore or be unaware of best practices (March, 1991).

Moreover, when pressure on teachers to implement particular curricula changes and to engage in issues of race using specific language, unlike the changing of gender-specific pronouns, a lack of structure is in place to support this shift. Consequently, teachers engage in higher levels of decoupling in the classroom and demonstrate little congruence with a protocol that seems different from organizational norms around other forms of difference in the community.

In the Fox Academy environment, using the concepts laid out by March (1991), the trade-offs between exploration and exploitation are a matter of short-term versus long-term impacts on community learning. March explores this through a model of mutual learning. Here, he describes learning in terms of organizational code, or agreed-upon truths and beliefs shared by organizational members, and how exploration and exploitation impact this learning (March, 1991).

By engaging in exploitation around issues of race, current practices are allowed to exist, creating a "garbage can" like in the *Adventures of Huckleberry Finn* scenario where solutions to problems are never fully addressed and tend to go away or simmer underneath the surface. Fox Academy greatly resembles society as a whole around issues of race. For organizations, the "garbage can" represents a model for describing and mapping various problems and solutions and the time and energy needed to solve those problems. Of the four essential variables, the energy and time of participants to engage in problem-solving and the rate and flow of solutions seem most notable here (Cohen, M. D., March, J. G., & Olsen, J. P., 1972). Despite Weick's (2001) assertion that the legitimation of doubt can have a beneficial and transformative impact on organization code, the lack of guidance around how sense is made of race continues to prevail in the Fox Academy community and Quaker schools as a whole.

Teachers understand that the returns from exploration around issues of race are less certain, perhaps more costly, and more challenging to measure in the school setting. Thus, they do not feel the same anxiety to conform to the pressure. Ultimately, Fox Academy resorts to ceremonial practices and high levels of decoupling and inertia as ways of protection from the uncertainty of racial pressures. As a result, the race concept gets addressed without being dealt with in the organization.

References

Rowan, B., & Miskel, C. G. (1999). Institutional theory and the study of educational organizations. In *Handbook of research on educational administration: A project of the American Educational Research Association* (Vol. 2, pp. 359–383).

Coburn, C. E. (2004). Beyond decoupling: Rethinking the relationship between the institutional environment and the classroom. *Sociology of Education, 77*(3), 211–244.

Hannan, M. T., & Freeman, J. (1984). Structural inertia and organizational change. *American Sociological Review, 49*(2), 149–164. Retrieved from http://www.jstor.org/stable/2095567

Meyer, J. W., & Rowan, B. (1977). Institutionalized organizations: Formal structure as myth and ceremony. *American Journal of Sociology, 83*(2), 340.

Fredrickson, H. G., & Smith, K. B. (2003). *The public administration theory primer* (Ch. 5 Theories of Public Management). Boulder, CO: Westview Press.

Blau, P. M. (1955). *The dynamics of bureaucracy: A study of interpersonal relations in two government agencies.* Chicago, IL: The University of Chicago Press.

March, J. G. (1991). Exploration and exploitation in organizational learning. *Organization Science, 2*(1), 71–87.

Cohen, M. D., March, J. G., & Olsen, J. P. (1972). A garbage can model of organizational choice. *Administrative Science Quarterly, 72*(1), 1–25.

Taylor, F. W. (1915/1981). Scientific management. In O. Grusky & G. A. Miller (Eds.), *The sociology of organizations.* New York, NY: The Free Press.

Weber, M. (1949/1993). Bureaucracy. In F. Fischer & C. Sirianni (Eds.), *Critical studies in organization and bureaucracy*. Philadelphia, PA: Temple University Press.

Pfeffer, J., & Salancik, G. R. (1978). *The external control of organizations: A resource dependence perspective*. Book, New York: Harper & Row.

Orton, J. D., & Weick, K. E. (1990). Loosely coupled systems: A reconceptualization. *The Academy of Management Review, 15*(2), 203–223.

Weick, K.E. (2001). *Making Sense of the Organization*. Malden, MA: Blackwell Publishing Ltd. 8(2), 91-102.

Lipsky, M. (1993). The rationing of services in street-level bureaucracies. In F. Fischer & C. Sirianni (Eds.), *Critical studies in organization and bureaucracy*. Philadelphia, PA: Temple University Press.

THE IMPACT OF THE HIRING AND RETENTION POLICY FOR TEACHERS OF COLOR AT ROOSEVELT SCHOOL

Macro-level Policy

The debate over who should control educational policy has never been more critical as standardized testing, the expansion of charter schools, and the inequity of the funding formula threaten to alter the trajectory of public education and its purpose for generations (Fowler, 2014). Moreover, sentiments about poor teaching, underprepared students, and school violence have ushered in policies at the Federal level that have rendered those with the most knowledge, teachers, and the least voice, also teachers, feeling powerless at both the implementation and evaluation stages of the policy process (Fowler, 2014).

The fluid nature of politics has created uncertainty as to the role of all actors involved in policy formation, and state and local agencies try as best they can to decouple from practices that they believe are detrimental to those they serve. At the same time, Federal agents continue to frame initiatives around student and teacher accountability levels. In addition, funding disagreements remain constant, with a shockingly small amount coming from the Federal Government and state and local level blame games about monetary mismanagement (Marion & Rogers, 2011).

Understanding how policy works, from the definition of the issue to the setting of the agenda, through policy formation and adoption and even the stages of implementation and evaluation, can be gained by the study of large-scale innovations like No Child Left Behind or Race to the Top legislation (Fowler, 2014). However, clarity can also come from more micro-level case studies of policy and how the actors in a community emulate the roles witnessed on macro level national policy. This paper will examine how Roosevelt Friends School's hiring and retention policy for teachers of color is supportive of social justice in wording but does not promote equity when being executed.

Micro-level Policy

Since 1938, Roosevelt Friends School has been steadfast in exploring all forms of diversity. It has tried to navigate a tricky balance between tuition-driven elitism and the Quaker principle of equality that guides the school. This struggle is as real in the pinnings of the institution now as at any time in the school's tenure, as tuition prices, marketing strategies and competition often compromise the mission and vision of the school. These environmental pressures have impacted how the school deals with conflicts involving the concept of racial equity in hiring. The answers gained by an inquiry about the school's hiring and retention protocol for teachers of color may prove vital in two ways. First, if Roosevelt Friends School's policy fails to increase the number of faculty of color, can organizational value or cost be measured from this? Secondly, does isolating the concept of race from how other needs of the institution get managed impact policy legitimacy in the constituencies' views.

Exploring the policy: Hiring and Retention of Teachers of Color

After decades of struggling to recruit and retain teachers of color, in 2013, Roosevelt Friends School set forth an agenda item to address the problem. A new policy would require that a teacher of color be a finalist in every teaching and administrative position that became available and that recruitment become the responsibility of a newly developed school role, Director of Hiring and Retention. These two steps of having a finalist mandate and accountability through paid responsibility were seemingly essential in the proposal that aimed to balance the diversity of the teaching faculty while supporting more marginalized student groups and parents.

The policy was verbally endorsed by teachers and administrators who felt the challenge of a more diverse student population. As a result, the Board of Trustees moved forward, believing that the stakeholders favored the shift in how hiring would take place on campus. The immediate impact of the policy change was noticeable with candidates of color more frequent on campus and an identifiable person that could address the concerns of students, teachers, and parents while working intentionally to improve the teacher of color demographic in the community.

The policy was reasonably clear in identifying the type of candidate of color that must be a finalist for any given position but left room for interpretation and autonomy in other ways that became problematic. In the words of the policy, the candidate must be "hireable" (Roosevelt Friends School, 2013). The language choice was in response to previous attempts to increase the population of teachers of color that resembled quotas and lacked legitimacy. There was no real possibility for employment.

Justification of the policy adoption spoke to the great need to increase the number of faculty of color placed in front of students. The framing of the policy notes that Black teachers, a percentage that has decreased significantly in the last three decades, typically choose to work in environments with higher numbers of children of color (Boser, 2014). However, in the most commonly cited research positing the benefits of teacher of color recruitment and retention, Dee (2005) points out the positive achievement outcomes in math and reading for children of color when being instructed by teachers of color.

Independent schools like Roosevelt Friends are servicing higher percentages of students of color, yet hiring teachers of color lag far behind (National Association of Independent Schools, 2017). Research also supported that increased teacher of color presence leads to better student attendance, higher placement in advanced classes, and decreased suspension and expulsion rates for students of color (Villegas & Irvine, 2010). These findings made the policy popular with parents and allowed the school to advertise such progressive practices to appear aligned with school values and competitors.

Policy Problems

Despite a policy with good intent and data-driven framing, the hiring and retention protocol has failed miserably. There are significant flaws in how the policy lives in the institution. It does not guard against personal preference or biases described in the "wrong fit" scenarios common in private schools. At the implementation stage, Department Chairs yield the majority of the power in the hiring process. Once candidates pass through the Director of Hiring and Retention, they still face this additional step to being hired that hinders faculty diversity progress and equity. As few people of color are present at the actual decision-making time for candidates that become finalists, perspectives are missing from the discourse that may help expand the lens of possibility. Moreover, candidates of color have few faces in the room that resemble them during the interviewing process, which may inadvertently and unfairly impact their comfort levels.

Another problem with the policy is that it fails to state how success is measured and does little if anything to support teachers of color once they become community members. Research suggests that teachers of color, like all other teachers, want supportive colleagues who are also available for "social interaction, reassurance, and psychological support" (Johnson, 1990, p. 156). Moreover, teachers of color, according to a study by Achinstein and Ogawa (2011), need culturally responsive colleagues and question their belonging to a given community when their respective cultural values lack acceptance. This is only further compromised when teachers of color in predominantly white institutions get less profitable or prestigious roles. At Roosevelt Friends School, the policy of hiring and retention does not account for the lack of supportive alliances for teachers of color, making their stay in the community uncomfortable and brief.

Changes to the policy

Changes to the hiring and retention of teachers of color must come in several ways. First, the policy requirement to have a teacher of color as a finalist must change, so the charge is to hire qualified teachers of color. This distinction is important because qualification does not mean the best based on the traditional value codes of the school (Orfield, G & Frankenberg, 2014). By valuing the diversity of the candidate and by being responsive to the needs of the students, the teacher of color candidacy gets elevated because their value expands to be more than just their control over curricula content (Dee, 2005). Much like having a diverse faculty is valued regarding gender, for the policy of hiring and retention to gain traction, traditional ways of evaluating candidates of color must be "unlearned" in favor of ones that support equity and inclusivity.

Secondly, Department Chairs must have a diminished role in the hiring process. This necessary change in the policy is vital because Department Chairs have a narrow view of how diversity lives in a community. They primarily examine the student experience from a curricula lens, considering the wealth of content knowledge a given candidate may bring to an interview. As they seldom have a balcony view that can understand the student experience as they navigate all of their classes on a given day, they may fail to realize that every teacher that stands as an information provider in front of students may look very similar.

Consequently, Divisional Principals should have an increased role in hiring because they have a better understanding of faculty makeup and complete student experience. Although this complicates the already busy schedule of Principals, it is a needed change to the policy and one that can structurally allow for more equitable results.

Third, the policy of hiring and retention of teachers of color must focus more heavily on retention. Teacher of color turnover is high in independent schools. The average tenure lasts only three years (NAIS, 2017). Turnover complicates an already difficult hiring process, and the number of teachers of color on campus never improves. In addition, prospective candidates rarely come in contact with other faculty members that look like them. A more robust retention policy would require structural changes in how support is provided. Mentoring teachers of color to ensure they have access to the social avenues of the community is paramount to their staying in the community (Dee, 2005). They must also be given tracks to advancement by receiving sponsorship from administrators (Johnson, 2006).

These support structures are pivotal because new teachers of color will have an advocate speaking for them when promotions become available. A top-down approach to retention requires support from the Board of Trustees and the Head of school as funding must be attached to this service. Mentors of teachers of color must receive compensation for this vital job, and with pay, schools can expect accountability for mentorship.

Finally, the resource or capital that Roosevelt Friends must secure most is that of students and tuition-paying parents. Empowering the voices of not only parents of students of color but those advocates for equity will place necessary pressure on the institution to produce results (Orr & Rogers, 2011). Parents carry leverage in the form of tuition dollars but often hesitate to use this carrot around issues of diversity. They must do so as they are emboldened to do around academic topics.

Figure 1.1 shows current aspects of the Policy for Hiring and Retention of Teachers of Color and what amendments are needed for more equitable practice and results.

Policy for Hiring and Retention of Teachers of Color	Current Policy	Change Needed & Possible Result
Candidates	Candidate of color as finalist	Hire qualified candidates of color even if they are not necessarily the strongest teachers (Value systems must be adjusted)
Hiring	Department Chairs and Committee	Division Principals have a balcony view of faculty profiles and the student experience
Retention	No differentiation between teachers of color and all other teachers	Teachers of color must have mentors and sponsors that provide social access and advancement opportunity
Framing of Issue	Done by the school on their terms	Done by students and parents based on educational and equity costs

Measuring success and accountability

Measuring hiring and retention success for teachers of color must be quantitative and qualitative (Dee, 2005). It is important to see growth in the number of teachers of color in front of students and in administrative positions. Cultural changes supporting retention are also valuable (Orfield & Frankenberg, 2014). Thus, Principals and Department Chairs must be held accountable for increasing the number of teachers of color at Roosevelt Friends School and creating an environment that supports retention. Students of color deserve to see themselves reflected in the classroom instructors. White students must engage with teachers of color as the authority and information providers for healthy social learning (Villages & Irvine, 2010). The policy's goal should be for the number of teachers of color to equal or exceed the percentage of students of color. Currently, that percentage stands at 35% of the population.

The retention measure must come through exit interviews with departing faculty of color and teachers remaining for longer than five years. Teachers of color who stay at the same independent school for five years remain for 20 or more years (NAIS, 2016). Thus, this five-year benchmark is crucial. A better understanding of the experience of teachers of color will benefit the entire community by expanding the perspective and empowering voice.

Conclusion

The policy of Hiring and Retention of Teachers of Color at Roosevelt Friends School sounds equitable in its wording. It addresses data-backed research that specifically points to the impact on students in and out of the classroom when exposed to diverse instructors. However, Roosevelt Friends School's policy has fallen short of the desired goal as it fails to offer institutional accountability for hiring while never addressing the environmental factors that weaken retention. Changes to the policy must come from internal and external pressures and target the Head of School and the Board of Trustees, demanding that they examine structures working counter to the policy's stated goals. Students and teachers must exercise their voice by continuously pointing to how lacking teachers of color diversity impacts academic outcomes and is inconsistent with the mission of the Quaker school.

Finally, parents must leverage tuition dollars in proven effective ways when lobbying for academic changes and assume the framing of the discussion about hiring and retention on their terms. As the policy for hiring and retaining teachers of color already exists, changes seem less daunting and create a level of optimism about the future.

References

Achinstein, B., & Ogawa, R. (2011). Change(d) agents: *New teachers of color in urban schools*. New York: Teachers College Press.

Boser, U. (2014). *Teacher diversity revisited: A new state-by-state analysis*. Center for American Progress. Retrieved from https://www.americanprogress.org/issues/race/report/2014/05/04/88962/teacherdiversity-revisited/

Dee, T. (2005). A teacher like me: Does race, ethnicity, or gender matter? *American Economic Review*, 95(2), 158–165.

Fowler, F. C. (2014). *Policy studies for educational leaders: an introduction*. Essex, England: Pearson Education Limited.

Johnson, S. M. (2006). The workplace matters: Teacher quality, retention, and effectiveness. Working Paper. *National Education Association Research Department*.

Orfield, G., & Frankenberg, E. (2014). *Brown at 60: Great progress, a long retreat and an uncertain future*. The Civil Rights Project, UCLA.

Orr, M., & Rogers, J. (2011). *Public engagement for public education: joining forces to revitalize democracy and equalize schools*. Stanford, CA: Stanford University Press.

Villegas, A. M., & Irvine, J. J. (2010). Diversifying the teaching force: An examination of major arguments. *The Urban Review*, 42(3), 175–192. http://doi.org/10.1007/s11256-010-0150- 1

ETHICAL LEADERSHIP:
CASE STUDY REVISITED

Introduction

There is no shortage of ethical decisions that educational leaders must make. The management of students, teachers, parents, and other constituencies with different needs and challenges is a complicated web requiring that problems be solved using various frameworks. In educational settings, decisions are often made with incomplete information, under time constraints, or through the limited lens of the leader's personal experience and positioning. When ethical decisions are required, this becomes even more complicated. Absent an appropriate approach to consider in these moments; the educational leader may find themselves relying too heavily on one ethical paradigm and not enough on another, unaware of the insight and perspective that may be missing. An ethical paradox happens when a person faces a decision with two logical solutions. The decision is complicated because it may simultaneously be helpful to some and hurtful to others. The ethical dilemma described in this paper, and now reconsidered many years later, looks at the paradox of race versus responsibility in a situation where my behavior, although seemingly justified at the time, now appears inauthentic to how I conduct myself as an ethical leader today.

Case Study (A)

I was in my fifth year of employment, having just earned my first administrative position as a Diversity Coordinator at a school. It was an important position for me and a job that I took seriously, wanting to address numerous issues of equity and injustice that seemed institutionalized on campus. Although I lacked professional experience, I felt life prepared me for this appointment. For most of my younger life, I have negotiated learning environments where I was one of a few students of color in a space and where the lack of diversity caused academic, social, and emotional challenges. In ways, I was energized by and felt charged to be a protector of those students traditionally and institutionally marginalized. They needed a voice in rooms where their opinions, views, and experiences often get discounted and silenced, and I felt that I had a platform to change this.

Ryan was a bright and energetic Black male student new to the school. He entered during a time when several other Black boys were unfortunately counseled out, some for reasons justified and others not. Often these decisions were couched in two ways; academic struggles or behaviors inconsistent with the community's norms. It had also become commonplace during re-enrollment meetings or times where the community of teachers discussed whether or not a student should return that the only faces that made a list and projected on the screen were that of kids of color and primarily Black boys. I could recall thinking that this practice was similar to the effects of police mug shots or the pictures of Black male faces that would flash on the news accompanied by some report of the terrible or heinous crime they had committed. For me, this practice had a dehumanizing impact and reinforced stereotypes and existing biases that make Black boys out to be the other and consequently feared.

However, Ryan was different, and after spending the first half of the year with this charismatic and charming young person, I started making plans as to how he would be instrumental in helping change how the community viewed Black boys. Ryan was not only bright and athletic but also a gifted musician, having self-taught himself how to play the piano, one of three instruments that he had seemingly mastered. He had also recently secured the lead in the school play, which no other student of color had done in years and a compliment to his years of study at a renowned acting school in town. His boundless diversity was what was needed to challenge the narrative on campus about Black boys. His being so brilliant and multidimensional was enough to counter inherited and negative "truths" about Black boys in the community.

My hope for Ryan to redirect the trajectory of Black boys in the community were compromised when he was accused of having inappropriate sexual contact with another student at an off-campus party. The female student reported to the school counselor that at a party where the students were drinking, Ryan touched her in private places on several occasions even after being asked to stop and forcefully, even if only momentarily, prohibited her from leaving a remote area at the party.

She told the counselor that she had flirted with Ryan since he had arrived at the school. However, at no time did she invite or ask for any physical contact, and she could recall telling Ryan to stop, once politely and another more aggressively, but to little success. Finally, she said that her threat to scream made Ryan move away from blocking her exit and that she and a friend quickly left the party afterward. Although it should not have mattered, the optics of the female being a white student seemed to magnify the situation on campus and did so internally for me, who was often the only Black male present in spaces to discuss and ponder Ryan's fate at the school.

The call for Ryan to be removed was immediate, and as word spread about what took place at the party and of the students involved, the divide was almost exclusively along racial lines. The female student was also in excellent standing at the school, having been appointed to several leadership positions and stood out in the classroom. The only criticism she ever received was what was considered by school standards as a more provocative style of dress. Her defenders pointed out that she dressed like the other female students, but her body shape made her outfits fit differently. I agreed that her dress style was inconsequential and highly offensive to introduce as a discussion point in the situation.

Black students and parents supported Ryan and feared that this was yet another message validating they were not welcomed in the community. Immediately, parents of color started reaching out to me for support and asking that I hold the school accountable for their biases and double standards around discipline.

To Ryan's credit, he admitted to the inappropriate touching of the female student, although he disputed the number of times he recalled being asked to stop. He misread the flirting that had been going on for weeks and even that evening at the party. The blocking of the exit was in question as he felt that she could have squeezed by at any moment. He was apologetic but said that the boys at school touched girls like that all the time, and he felt that his behavior, although wrong, fell far short of the vitriol spewed throughout campus. He, like his family, attributed this to racism, claiming that if Ryan was a white boy, expulsion would not be an option, although the situation would need addressing.

The Paradox: Race versus Responsibility

The paradox for me in the situation was that I felt a huge responsibility to protect Ryan as a Black male student from the history of racial bias at the school, but also to be steadfast in support of holding the line around all forms of sexual harassment. Sexual harassment, and its many forms, also had a dubious history in the school and society, and even according to Ryan, it was still acceptable and tolerated in student spaces.

Once Ryan was temporarily suspended so all information could be vetted and processed, I spoke passionately at meetings about why he should be allowed to return to school. Much of what I offered was pertinent to the school's relationship with race and how this impacted those calling for Ryan's expulsion. Despite learning that another student, a Black female, had witnessed Ryan blocking the doorway and the appearance of the white female student walking away, my need to challenge a school's history of racial injustice seemed significant. Perhaps this seemed greater than my care for another student who was the victim.

I believe that I guilted those responsible for deciding to allow Ryan to return by questioning their racism in ways that were perhaps unfair in this case. In retrospect, Ryan became the beneficiary of years of unfair treatment of Black boys, but at the expense of a white female student and perhaps her first encounter with sexual harassment.

Ultimately, Ryan was allowed to return with a two-week suspension, but the female student withdrew from the school, feeling that the community failed to protect her. Her family would go on to sue the school and eventually settle. Although Ryan finished his tenure at the school in good standing and earned placement in a prestigious university, he failed to learn his lesson. After his first year, he was expelled with several friends for recording and sharing a video of a sexual encounter with another girl.

Ethical Reflection (B) and Turbulence Theory

Turbulence theory posits that gauges can measure the level of disturbance associated with a given situation. This advantage is that measuring turbulence allows leaders to appropriately respond to a given problem using reasoned action, not driven by emotions or the chaos of the moment. The four gauges, as described by Shapiro & Gross (2013), consider light, moderate, severe, and extreme as indicators that should influence the leader's decisions and actions. Additionally, turbulence theory considers the decision maker and their positioning in the disturbance and encourages that person to consider the positioning of others in the situation. As all turbulence is not experienced in the same way or even at the same time for all members of a situation, understanding positioning from a multidimensional lens seems essential.

In the case described, the turbulence for me settled between moderate and severe on the gauge (Shapiro & Gross, 2013). Whereas the turbulence felt was most significant for the students involved in the situation, reaching what I would consider extreme, my positioning as an adult whose future in the community was not in jeopardy provided certain protections against professional cascading. Also, although I felt tremendous pressure from parents and students of color to represent them fairly, the final decision was joint, with many administrators involved. Finally, although I believe it to have been significant, my input needed the institutional validation of more senior administrators. Consequently, they needed to provide the language to explain the decision to the young girl, her family, and the rest of the community.

(C) Table 1.1: Turbulence Gauge My Positioning in the Situation

Degree of Turbulence	General Definition	Turbulence as Applied to Situation
Moderate	Widespread awareness of the issue, specific origins	Racial divides are noticeable on campus and pressure is felt to represent those with silenced voices
Severe	Fear for the entire enterprise, possibility of large-scale community demonstration, a feeling of crisis	The school administration appears to demonstrate little concern for issues of sexual harassment threatening the emotion safety of many students. The reputation of the school is harmed

Table 2.1: Turbulence Gauge for Female Student

Extreme	Things seem to be falling apart	The female student feels that she is no longer safe because of the student who harassed her but also because the school fails to protect her. She feels the need to remove herself from friends, teachers, and the community and questions if it was worth it to report the abuse or if she will ever report such forms of harassment again.

(D) The Ethical Paradigms

Ethic of Care

Central to the ethic of care is the understanding that decisions that are made will impact the people involved in a situation differently (Shapiro & Gross, 2013). It considers the various impacts that may harm some while intentionally or unintentionally helping or benefiting others. This is not to suggest that because the consequences in a given situation may not appear to be equitable-- that they are unjust, the ethic of care is about the purposeful consideration of how all people, because of their positioning in the situation, may be impacted (Shapiro & Gross, 2013).

Also, crucial to understanding the ethic of care is being guided by and responsive to the needs of people. Questions that ask that you consider the long term effects of the decisions being made help to extend the lens of consequences that may ultimately be felt by those involved. Mainly, the ethic of care seems to work to humanize all people in a situation, even when it may be easier and less emotionally demanding to box them into categories of good and bad, right and wrong, and just and unjust, so that attempts at being responsive to their needs is possible.

In the case study here, like in many complicated decisions that are made during the school year, the ethic of care was demonstrated in the consideration of how Ryan might be impacted if removed from the community. The consideration of students, along racial lines, and concerning the historically advantaged and disadvantaged in the community, ushered in conversations about how the school has often failed to be responsive to the needs of certain marginalized groups. Care was demonstrated by thinking long term and in understanding interesting correlations between school discipline and direct lines to prison, especially in regards to Black males. However, the ethic of care was not as obvious as it pertained to the female student who reported the harassment. Although the school counselor reacted as needed by reporting the information he received to administrators and in his support of the student and family through the process, how she would be impacted long term did not garner the same attention. What she needed in the moment, assurances that she was safe, people in place for her to turn to, validation that she was doing the right thing by reporting what happened to her, lost credibility once her personal experience as the victim of harassment seemed to be dwarfed by the narrative of racial bias and prejudice that attached itself to the situation.

Ethic of Justice

The ideas of fairness and equality resonate from the ethic of justice and the consideration of laws and policies that must be used to guide practice (Shapiro & Gross, 2013). It also requires the pondering of how the rules and policies are ultimately implemented. Complicating the ethic of justice are those situations that may not be guided by clear rules or policies but that still require the standard of fairness. This aspect is perhaps more subjective as perspectives and opinions around issues of equity are not uniform. There was no formal charge of sexual harassment brought against Ryan in a court of law, nor did his actions take place on school grounds. To the school's credit, they did not back away from dealing with the situation as an institution although they could have done so by law, forcing the female student and her family to seek justice through the courts. School policy required that the family be informed of the situation between the students and that they are given full authority to pursue any avenue to justice that they desired.

Ethic of Critique

Redefining concepts, challenging power and privilege and empowering and giving voice to those silenced are considered when using the ethic of critique (Shapiro & Gross, 2013). This may have been the ethical paradigm most prominent in the case study. The challenging of power and privilege that is often systemic in private schools and the empowering of silenced voices of students of color and their parents permeated this situation. Through the ethic of critique, flaws in the practices that unfairly penalize kids of color were identified and led to new initiatives that allowed the school to be more reflective of systemic biases. However, not enough attention was given to the culture of harassment that had been discovered as some boys seemed to treat female students with disrespect and their experiences with nonchalance. Whereas discrepancies in racial power in the community were highlighted, caution was used in illuminating the power difference between males and females in the ranks of students and adults. The discovery of lax harassment descriptions in the student handbook did not sound the alarms in the community that there was a problem. Although through the ethic of critique some improvements were ignited for females and harassment, this did not come with the same urgency as issues that involved race.

Ethic of the Profession

The ethic of the profession asks that the consideration of what is best for students guide the decision-making (Shapiro & Gross, 2013). There is perhaps nothing more important to educators than the protection of children; as the case study demonstrates, this drives the decision-making in specific ways. The school administration considered that a suspension of Ryan was in his best interest, protecting his future and hoping that through education around the issue of harassment, they were holding to professional codes of students learning through their errors. In my case, my professional goals included making the school more intellectually diverse by expanding the lens of understanding about students of color in the school. This goal included being in a position to bring about change and challenge authority when given the opportunity. However, the profession's ethic intends for leaders' views to be greater and to consider what is best for all students, not just a few (Shapiro & Gross, 2013). In the case study, what was in the best interest of the female student, her family, and a community having to engage with the nuances of harassment, may have fallen short.

Discussion of the Dilemma

In Chmielewski's (2004) work, she notes that as part of her three-point system, a balance between benefits and burden must be achieved to arrive at a decision. She suggests that the benefit from the decision must outweigh the burden. Concerning Ryan, the benefit of being able to return to school was not greater than the burden felt by the community after his return. Female students and others began to question their safety in the community, and the loss of a student victim of harassment signaled that the school was ill-prepared for these challenges. An examination of Lashway's (2006) questions to guide ethical decision-making hints that student learning depends on feeling valued. Schaps (1998) explanation of the risks and rewards of community building urges administrators to be courageous enough to do what is best for those students most in need. In this case, the brave decision might have been to remove Ryan and not to sacrifice what is perhaps the most crucial variable that schools can provide to children, safety.

It is essential to note the reality of many Black males in the educational system. Even when removing factors of poverty and dealing with students demonstrating high academic achievement, Black students get disciplined at a higher level than their white counterparts (Anyon et al., 2014; Simmons, Feggins, & Chung, 2005). Bradshaw et al. (2010) offered that racial prejudices get internalized in young people during the ages of five to ten and that their views on negative and positive characteristics and the placement of people into good and bad categories may be difficult to change after this point. Therefore, it was appropriate to be aware of information concerning how Black students navigate school and society. Recognizing the biases that their actions and behaviors often illicit (Blake et al., 2011) is necessary, but countering destructive trends must not come by removing power from other marginalized groups.

Rethinking the Decision

My experience handling difficult decisions has been sharpened by considering and adopting certain ethical paradigms. Most decisions are difficult but using ethical paradigms provides perspective and clarity concerning Ryan and the female student many years ago. I now consider my role in the situation to be less ethical and even less authentic to who I am as a leader and person today. In retrospect, the school should have illuminated the experience of the female victim. Her protection should have been protected by those charged with this responsibility. Although Ryan deserved care, the critique used to challenge the school around racially sensitive issues now seems problematic. I did not frame the intersection of race and gender appropriately.

It has been challenging to reconcile this case study over the years. There are two aspects of my decision-making that I question, both raising ethical issues for me. First, my positioning as a Black male teacher may have biased my rhetoric in such a way that unfairly emphasized Ryan's race more than the female student that got harassed. By connecting the history of racial intolerance, and how this lives in most institutions, this may have been a distraction from the focus being where it needed, the issue of sexual harassment of a student.

Although the use of the ethical paradigms is more about the process than outcomes, as a human, I struggle with the fact that Ryan, who had an opportunity to grow from this experience, became involved in another abuse situation in college. Also, the white female student who was a victim felt the need to leave her learning community, further bringing the idea of equity into question. From what I have learned of her since her departure, she went on to college and law school, yet there is no way of me knowing the situation's impact on her emotional health. I question my professional motives in this situation as well, wondering if I was ethically compromised by not wanting to appear to Black students and parents as some "sell-out" by not supporting what was popular opinion.

Finally, if this situation were to occur today, I would be mindful of the care that both students need, which might require removing Ryan from the community. I would do all possible for him and his family to find another school and help to secure the appropriate counseling. It would also be vital for me to speak the truth about the situation by ensuring that the work needed in the community around race and justice would not be confused with what was right and required to protect a female sexual harassment victim. By conflating the two, there would remain the risk that the school might lose sight of what is perhaps most important in a situation of sexual harassment and risk victimizing the victim. In some ways, I believe that my actions did this to the female student. Not enough care was given to her and her well-being.

References

Anyon, Y., Jenson, J. M., Aitchul, I., Farrar, J., McQueen, J., Greer, E., ... Simmons, J. (2014). The persistent effect of race on the promise of alternatives to suspension in school discipline outcomes. *Children and Youth Services Review*, 44, 379-386. Doi: 10.1016/j.childyouth.2014.06.025

Bradshaw, C. P., Mitchell, M. M., O'Brennan, L. M., Leaf, P. J. (2010). Multilevel exploration of factors contributing to the overrepresentation of black students in office disciplinary Referrals. *Journal of Educational Psychology*, 102, 508-520. Doi: 10.1037/a0018450

Blake, J. J., Butler, B. A., Lewis, C., & Darensbourg, A. (2011). Unmasking the inequitable Discipline experiences of urban Black girls: Implications for educational stakeholders. *The Urban Review*, 43, 90-116. Doi: 10. 1007/ s11256-009-0148-8

Chmielewski, C., (2004).The Importance of Values and Culture in Ethical Decision Making.Retrieved - from NACADA *Clearinghouse of Academic Advising Resources Web*

Lashway, L. (2006). Ethical leadership. In S. C. Smith and P. K. Piele (Eds.), School leadership: *Handbook for excellence in student learning* (4th ed). Thousand Oaks, CA: Corwin Press.

Schaps, E. (1998, September/October). Risks & rewards of community building. Thrust for *Educational Leadership*, 28(1), 6-9.

Shapiro, J. P., Gross, J. S. (2013). *Ethical Educational Leadership in Turbulent Times (Re)Solving Moral Dilemmas* (2nd ed). New York, NY: Routledge.

THE HIRING URGENCY

In *To Kill A Mockingbird*, Atticus Finch delivers in his closing remarks a compelling defense of the African American, Tom Robinson, a man accused of raping the white Mayella Ewell. However, instead of feebly attempting to save Tom, whose guilt is decided the moment he is accused, the morally sound Atticus puts the bigoted society of Maycomb on trial. Atticus, the hero, believes that he has the power to create a place where all are equal, a space where "a pauper is the equal of a Rockefeller...." But Atticus, the human, reveals that people create the society, and it is through this imperfection that such an idealistic utopia fails.

My experience as one of a few people of color to be called an independent school teacher is a story of far more highs than lows. It is also a story that mirrors the complexity of the character Atticus, the hero, and the human side of who we are. I share my story as my school embarks upon new initiatives designed to increase the diversity of teachers and administrators. Unfortunately, in my opinion, few endeavors align more with the school's Statement of Diversity and Inclusivity or with Quaker beliefs.

When asked how my experience differs from any of my white colleagues for this article, I chose not to write about often being the only person of color in a meeting. Nor will I consider the struggles I have faced around student fear or the constant pressure I feel to address stereotypes. I save for another time the difficulty experienced needing to be the voice around all diversity issues or the pressure felt to support all families of color. This is also not the moment for considering the professional boxes that have been nearly impossible to escape or the racially driven questioning of my abilities by parents and colleagues alike. Instead, I tell my story through two very different experiences. Separately, perhaps they say very little about the need for a more diverse faculty, but collectively, I believe that they underscore this necessity.

Several years ago, middle school teachers and students gathered in the auditorium because of a potential security threat. The principal at the time read a description provided to him by the local police of an African American man who had allegedly robbed a nearby store and was potentially hiding on or near campus. Despite the description including such details relating to height and hair (the latter I have none of), after the meeting, a group of students surrounded me and asked if I had committed the crime. We are human.

I believe this is a hiring issue because it was far too easy for these students to connect specific dots that never should have connected. Simply because they had no other point of reference, perhaps because of lack of exposure, I, a teacher in high standing, became instantly connected to a deviant based on skin color alone. I ask if they would have been able to make the same cognitive leap if the description was the same but referenced a white man?

Years later, after being appointed to my first administrative position for the school, I walked into an upper school faculty meeting ready to challenge all the injustices I believed were on campus. Full of passion but lacking perspective, my attack on those I would soon call friends was divisive, accusatory, and counterproductive to what would eventually reveal a shared goal. After the meeting, a colleague asked that I take a walk with him around campus. He taught me the most valuable lesson I have used in my work. The message was that truth and perspective were fluid and that I would need to model the type of understanding I expected from others to change a community. We are heroes.

It would take years to repair the damage done at that meeting. Looking back, I have questioned if our lack of faculty diversity empowered my voice so much that day. If other people of color were present to challenge my view, would my words have meant as much?

Like many other independent schools, my school faces challenges with hiring and retaining teachers of color. However, we have successfully acquired other forms of diversity in our faculty. Teachers come from different geographic areas, across socio-economic lines, have a primary language other than English, and identify as LGBTQ. These forms of diversity enhance our community, mirror the world beyond our campus, and allow our students to see themselves in the individuals who stand before them daily. They are both mirrors and windows.

But the obstacles we have faced in securing more teachers of color have proven to be worthy adversaries. Unfortunately, the results have fallen short of our desires and needs, be it insufficient pay, the lack of interest from candidates, shortcomings in how and where we post positions, or other unknown factors.

School practices targeting college and community outreach address this critical issue more intentionally, as well as hiring protocol that looks explicitly for diverse candidates. A regional Diversity Board is also committed to being current on the best strategies to attract qualified candidates of color. Perhaps most importantly, independent schools are prepared to examine any institutional barriers that may work against this goal.

After Tom Robinson is found guilty of the crime of rape, Atticus, the hero sees progress in the jury taking longer than usual to render their verdict. However, Atticus, the human, understands that progress is often a slow process that may even appear stagnant at times. Nevertheless, the Maycomb society is less damaged than first believed, and the astute reader can find myriad heroes, each doing their part to create a more perfect community.

There is no guarantee that our ambitious diversity initiatives will produce more faculty of color at our school or any other independent school. What is certain is that we must exhaust every possible resource available to move this pendulum forward.

www.ingramcontent.com/pod-product-compliance
Lightning Source LLC
Chambersburg PA
CBHW031324290526
45784CB00014B/1294